Why Temperament Matters

**Other Redleaf Press Books by Cindy Croft**

*Caring for Young Children with Special Needs* (Redleaf Quick Guide)

# Why Temperament Matters

Guidance Strategies for Young Children

Cindy Croft

**Redleaf Press®**
www.redleafpress.org
800-423-8309

Published by Redleaf Press
10 Yorkton Court
St. Paul, MN 55117
www.redleafpress.org

First edition 2021
Cover design by Renee Hammes
Cover photographs © Adobe Stock
Interior design by Douglas Schmitz
Typeset in ITC Stone Serif and Bell Centennial
Printed in the United States of America
28  27  26  25  24  23  22  21          1  2  3  4  5  6  7  8

Library of Congress Cataloging-in-Publication Data

Names: Croft, Cindy, author.
Title: Why temperament matters : guidance strategies for young children / by Cindy Croft.
Description: First edition. | St. Paul, MN : Redleaf Press, 2021. | Includes bibliographical references and index. | Summary: "This book provides specific ideas about how a child care provider can adjust the early childhood program and environment to meet the individual needs of each child's temperament. There is a specific emphasis on children who fall into the feisty/spirited or the slow-to-warm-up/sensitive categories because they are often the ones who are expelled with challenging behaviors. *Why Temperament Matters* explains where challenging behaviors may originate in temperament and provides strategies for meeting temperament needs that prevent or lessen challenging behaviors"— Provided by publisher.
Identifiers: LCCN 2020043139 (print) | LCCN 2020043140 (ebook) | ISBN 9781605546599 (paperback) | ISBN 9781605546605 (ebook)
Subjects: LCSH: Preschool children. | Temperament in children. | Behavioral assessment of children. | Child care services. | Early childhood education.
Classification: LCC HQ774.5 .C76 2021  (print) | LCC HQ774.5  (ebook) | DDC 155.42--dc23
LC record available at https://lccn.loc.gov/2020043139
LC ebook record available at https://lccn.loc.gov/2020043140

Printed on acid-free paper

# Contents

# Acknowledgments

I want to thank the editors at Redleaf Press for encouraging me to move forward with the idea for this book. I especially want to thank Kara Lomen for her positive energy! Thanks to Stephanie Schempp for guiding me through the editing process with wise direction.

I want to thank my colleagues at Concordia University, St. Paul's College of Education, especially Dr. Lynn Gehrke and Dr. Sue Starks, for all I have learned from them about young children.

To my own children, Melissa, Kimberly, and Matt, whose unique and individual temperaments have been a joy to watch unfold over all the years. To my husband, Don, who supports me every day in seeking understanding of the differences in all of us.

To Penelope, Harriet, Edmond, Isaac, Sam, Luke, Ethan, and Noah, who have the best yet in front of them and for whom I hope only the most wonderful world that honors each of them just because of who they are.

# Introduction

Children come to us with a natural wiring that comes partly from genetics and partly from the environment around them. We can't fundamentally change the disposition of a child, nor would we want to. Every child is unique, and it is in this uniqueness that we find so much to celebrate. Honoring every child is the work of early childhood. We want all children with their diverse dispositions to know that belonging is not just about attending our programs but about expressing vital and necessary parts of themselves. Everyone matters and everyone has a unique and equally important role to play in our child care communities.

In my years of work in early childhood, I have seen children who struggled to belong and providers who, in turn, struggled to include all children. Children keep the stamps we put on them in these early years. If they are repeatedly moved from program to program, they can begin to believe they are a bit less worthy than their peers. They can accept external statements that they are too busy or not a good fit and internalize those judgments. Providers, too, can feel a sense of failure because they couldn't meet a child's needs. Often what becomes identified as challenging behavior is the nature of the child, waiting to be nurtured and guided. My hope is that this book will give providers the tools to better support who children naturally are.

## Strategies and Temperament Traits

Chapters 3 through 11 are laid out exactly the same, each one highlighting a specific temperament trait. There is a definition of the trait as well as short vignettes throughout each chapter highlighting a child with that specific temperament trait. Each chapter examines a trait through the lens of its impact on a child's behavior, from high to low. For instance, low activity in energy would mean a child engages with less enthusiasm, whereas a child on the high activity end of the energy range would exhibit more zeal in actions and reactions. These chapters also look at positive and challenging behaviors related to each trait. Each chapter examines how a temperament trait influences relationships with adults and peers as well as how it affects play and other development. Each chapter contains strategies for individualizing programming as well as guidance strategies for a child demonstrating dominance in one of the temperament traits. Strategies will vary depending on the common challenges associated with a particular temperament trait. There are also some temperament traits that are not typically associated with challenging behaviors, and strategies for those include more positive approaches. Each chapter about a temperament trait ends with a story of success based on a child who has been positively included in child care.

## Usage of Terms

I use the terms *early childhood educator, child care provider, caregiver,* and *teacher* interchangeably to refer to the same professional in the early childhood field. *Child care program, classroom, early education program, early childhood setting,* and *family child care* are also used interchangeably to refer to the setting where children are cared for and educated from birth through preschool age outside of the family home.

All children's names are fictitious and represent a composite of children I have known over the years. All child care programs are also fictitious and also represent aspects of programs I have seen or heard about through the Center for Inclusive Child Care, an inclusion coaching program in St. Paul, Minnesota. The pronouns *he* and *she* are used interchangeably throughout this book and do not indicate that certain temperament traits are more prevalent by gender.

# 1

# Why Temperament Matters!

Every child care program has a unique blend of children, from the extroverted daredevil to the quiet teacher pleaser. Our classrooms reflect the world around us. The diversity of personalities is what makes early education challenging and fun at the same time, while teachers say this is the job they love!

What makes every child so unique? No matter the size of a child care program, there will be children who want to be the center of attention and those who prefer to quietly play in the reading nook. Children come into this world with their own wiring that is influenced partly by genetics and partly by the environment around them. We refer to all the characteristics that make up a child's personality as her temperament. Temperament is the predisposition we are all born with, and it colors the way we react to the world around us. My definition is "the characteristic way that the individual experiences and responds to the internal and external environment" (Croft 2007, 43). Temperament is innate and part of who we are from birth.

Because temperament is present at birth, an infant will show personality characteristics that become recognizable as part of her overall nature as she grows. For example, an infant might be resistant to a sleeping schedule in her early weeks. A few years later, that same preschooler may have difficulty in child care when snacktime comes and she isn't hungry for another half hour. The infant's emerging personality can be seen as a small seed, and nurturing and support from her primary caregiver helps the child grow successfully into the unique person she was born to be.

Why does temperament matter to you as an early educator? For one thing, everyone has temperament traits. Every child you care for comes to you with different combinations of nine temperament traits. The temperament traits a child has influence every part of her child care day, from when she arrives, to lunch, to when she goes home at the end of the day. For instance, if a child is hungry before everyone else in the class, hunger may make her irritable and unwilling to share with a friend. Or if she has difficulty persisting in a table activity, she may become disruptive in order to make a change.

> While everyone else is napping or lying quietly on their mats, Lionel can't stop fidgeting and moving his feet around. He just has to touch the friend lying next to him. His little body doesn't slow down the way others' bodies do at quiet time.

As educators and providers, the more you know about an individual child's temperament traits, the better equipped you are to adapt the environment to accommodate her physical, behavioral, and learning needs. The purpose of this book is to explain how each of the nine temperament traits can affect a child's behavior in child care and offer strategies for building success for both children and providers. Building a sense of mastery for everyone in the classroom promotes a positive environment!

## Understanding Temperament Traits

Broadly speaking, the components that make up the personality and disposition of children and adults is known as temperament. For instance, a child's personality might be energetic and outgoing, with temperament traits like high activity level and high approach. The individual nine temperaments go together to give each person their unique personality. We will talk in more depth about temperament traits in the next section. It is sometimes thought that temperament is changeable over time, but in fact it is fairly stable from infancy into adulthood. A child with high intensity will not become a child who shows little or no reaction to his world, but that child can learn skills in early childhood to help regulate some of his reactions. Temperament is influenced by environment, which is why the early education setting plays an important role in how temperament manifests in child care. One example of this is a child care setting that uses muted colors, dims the lights at times, and puts quiet centers next to other quiet centers. These calming influences help a child who can be overstimulated by a noisy or active environment, allowing her to stay on a more even keel.

There are other influences on temperament as well, such as stressors in a child's life that cause anxiousness in a child who might otherwise be adaptable.

Our culture tends to view boys as more active and girls as more social, but these traits in individual children have more to do with genetics than culture or gender. Social relationships will have some influence on behaviors, but they will not fundamentally alter a temperament type. For instance, two friends who are working on a project together will work longer if one of them has higher persistence. It doesn't mean the other child will stay until the end, but she may remain longer than if she had been at the task alone.

Temperament is made up of nine specific traits first categorized in the 1970s by Stella Chess and her husband, Alexander Thomas, psychiatrists who studied child development over a period of several years, particularly temperament and environment. In their research, they measured each trait as high, low, or somewhere in the middle on a continuum on a temperament sorter. Sorters are a way to sequence the traits in an order. An example of a temperament sorter is found later in this chapter. Using a sorter helps you determine where you think a particular child's temperament traits tend to land on the continuum.

## The Nine Temperament Traits

When you examine all the temperament traits together, you see that they form a unique picture of each child with his own way of interacting with his environment. These are the nine traits:

1. **Activity level** is the overall physical energy a child uses in daily activities. How active is the child from an early age? Does he tend to be very busy most of the time or tend toward quiet activities? Was he a wiggly baby or one that nestled in and liked to be swaddled?

2. **Distractibility** refers to how difficult or easy it is for a child to concentrate without being sidetracked. How well does he pay attention if he's not particularly interested? Can his attention be diverted easily, or does he stay concentrated on a task? Does he want you to read every page of the book and notice if you skip any parts of it?

3. **Persistence** describes a child's ability to stick with a task in the face of distractions, interruptions, or frustration. Does the child stay with something he doesn't really like to do? If it becomes difficult, does he stay with it or move to the next game? Will he work on a challenging puzzle until he figures it out?

4. **Adaptability** is about how easily a child adjusts to changes in situations or people. How does the child deal with transitions or changes in routine? Does he roll with it or make a fuss when it is time to move to a new

activity? As an infant, did he go with the flow no matter what was happening? Or did he only sleep in his own bed with his own blankets?

5. **Approach/withdrawal** is about a child's first reaction to new situations or people. What is the child's initial response to newness? What is his reaction to new foods, places, activities, people, and clothes? Does he eagerly approach a new friend or tend toward hesitancy about new people? Does she hold back until she is sure about something?

6. **Intensity** refers to the energy a child uses to respond or react. How loud is the child, whether happy or unhappy? How much energy does he use to express joy, anger, or frustration? As an infant, was he hard to soothe and easily agitated?

7. **Regularity** is about the predictability of the child in his patterns of sleep, appetite, or bodily functions. Does he usually sleep at the same time each day, or is his napping time all over the place and unpredictable?

8. **Sensory threshold** is related to how sensitive a child is to her physical surroundings. How does the child react to sensory stimulation: noise, light, colors, smells, pain, tastes, and textures in clothing and food? Is he overstimulated or bothered by different sensations? Or does he show little reaction to sensory stimulation like a loud noise?

9. **Mood** is a child's general tendency to react positively or negatively to the world around him. What is the child's predominant mood? Is he more generally positive or negative?

## Challenges to Child Care Providers

Child developmentalists know that this natural composition of temperament traits is important because it can influence the trajectory of a child's ongoing positive social-emotional development through her relationship with a primary caregiver. For instance, a child who displays temperament traits that might be perceived as challenging, such as high activity level, could receive fewer positive interactions and more negative reactions from her caregiver. When this happens, the child may feel like there is something wrong with who she is because she senses caregivers' disapproval to her general busyness.

If a child persistently feels like she is being rejected by her provider or by peers, she could begin a downward spiral that continues to lower her sense of worth and sets a pattern for negative behaviors. The challenging behaviors will then continue to negatively impact interactions with her teachers, reinforcing the negative view she has of herself.

Since Albert gets in trouble so much anyway, what is the point of trying to do what the teacher says? He might as well see if he can get sent to the director's office because at least when he is there, she lets him feed the fish.

Conversely, if a child is highly approachable, her caregiver may smile at her frequently and give her positive encouragement for her positive attitude. The child can internalize this as "I must be okay because my teacher really likes me." For this child, the stage is being set for a positive future.

## Temperament Ranges and Clusters

The nine temperament traits above are further classified as having a range and presenting in a cluster of similar traits. Each temperament trait as a stand-alone characteristic has dimensions of impact on a child that we refer to as a "range," or area of variation. While *range* speaks to each individual trait, *clusters* refer to the traits that have characteristics in common or are related in range of high or low impact. In this way, we can better understand the whole nature of a child's personality expressed through their behaviors.

### Temperament Ranges

The impact of a particular temperament trait on a child's behavior can depend on what we refer to as its "range." Temperament range indicates whether the trait is experienced by the child with a high impact or low impact or even somewhere in the middle. For instance, if a child is on the high side of intensity, then we will see behaviors that represent strong self-expression, like loud talking and laughing, or big gestures of unhappiness or joy. He might throw himself on the ground with anger or scream with delight.

> Ruby bangs her cup on the table when she puts it down and marches instead of walking. Everything she does, she does BIG. Sometimes her peers aren't sure how to react to her because she can seem scary to them when she shouts or screams. Even when she is happy, she laughs louder than anyone else in the room.

If a child is low in how he expresses intensity, we may see behaviors that are not reactive in the way we would typically expect from a given age range. For instance, a child with low intensity might ignore a friend who hollers at him to hand over the red fire engine. He might react with little energy to a birthday surprise that would make most other children very excited. His emotions are subdued even if he is frustrated or angry.

Gil watches the magician do a magic trick in front of him but doesn't seem surprised when the toy reappears in the box. He turns away and starts to play with a squishy ball in his pocket.

There is no wrong or right, good or bad in temperament or range; it is simply the way a child is naturally wired to react based on that temperament trait. As we will see in chapters 3 through 11, the child's reactions can result in behaviors that are challenging unless there is guidance from adults and an environment that supports positive behaviors.

## Temperament Clusters

Temperament clusters or types are groupings of dominant temperament traits. Dominant traits are the ones that override the other dispositions of a child. Every child has all nine temperament traits, and each one has those traits clustered in some meaningful way. Thomas and Chess were the first to identify these personality types based on infants they were observing in a long-term study (Allen and Cowdery 2012). They noticed through the infant's behaviors a tendency for temperament traits to cluster or group depending on high impact, low impact, or middle-range impact. This is how they determined the three basic temperament types of classifications we still use today:

- Difficult (sometimes described as feisty or active)

- Easy (sometimes described as flexible or easygoing)

- Slow to warm up (sometimes described as fearful)

Chess and Thomas found that flexible or easy babies tended to be active but not to a degree that it was problematic for adults to care for them. They also found that the easy baby had calmer reactions when the unexpected occurred. Infants in this category tended to be "happy and contented" (quoted in Allen and Cowdery 2012, 391). The feisty or difficult category of temperament described an infant who was easily upset and resistant to change. This infant tended to fuss and cry more often than other infants. In addition, his biological regulation for eating, elimination, and sleeping was irregular, making it difficult for him to settle into a routine of care.

> Difficult babies are likely to be irritable, easily upset, and vigorously resistant to the unfamiliar. They cry more frequently, and they cry in a way that grates on parents' and caregivers' ears (and nerves). Biological rhythms (eating, sleeping, and elimination patterns) are difficult to regulate. . . .

Slow-to-warm-up infants show few intense reactions, either positive or negative. They seldom are outright resistant to new experiences, but neither are they eager to sample the unknown. For example, instead of fighting off a new food, they may simply not swallow it. . . . Passive resistant is a term used to describe this type of behavior (Allen and Cowdery 2012, 391).

About 40 percent of the sample done by Thomas and Chess categorized children as easy or flexible. From early on, these children tend to be well regulated in sleep and eating patterns and are generally happy and tend to go with the flow. Again according to the sample, 10 percent of children tend toward feisty or active, with higher degrees of irregularity and lower adaptability to change. Fifteen percent are in the category of slow to warm up, with a more negative mood and a harder time adjusting to change. Child developmentalist Laura E. Berk (2013) notes that 35 percent of all children do not fit clearly into one category but instead have temperament traits that are uniquely blended.

## Common Temperament Types

All of us, from infants to adults, have a collection of temperament traits that tend to determine if we are generally a go-with-the-flow, stand-back-and-wait, or hit-life-head-on type of person. Once you understand this, you can see where behaviors related to temperament traits can be challenging at times in different situations. In subsequent chapters, this book will lay out behaviors that might result from each specific temperament trait and will include strategies for making environmental and programmatic changes to modify those behaviors. First we will look at some behaviors specific to the three temperament types: flexible, feisty, and fearful.

### Flexible

The first temperament type is what many early educators might wish they had a classroom full of: flexible, easy temperaments! Children who are easygoing tend to be happy from birth and adjust easily to change. A child who is flexible tends to be a child with temperament traits that are easy to work with. This cluster of traits includes the following:

- A higher level of adaptability, which means the child transitions easily and will make changes without a fuss; a higher level of adaptability means the child probably doesn't demand very much from their caregiver

- A higher approach, which means the child will meet new children quickly and make friends with them; the child will welcome peers right away

- A positive view of what is going on around them

Because children are young and are learning through experiencing the world, there will always be behavior mistakes and mishaps, no matter the ease of the child's personality. Social competence is learned through trial and error in play with peers, but the flexible child will be less likely to exhibit the challenging behaviors that can be so difficult for child care providers, like aggression or overactivity.

> Ms. Jennifer pairs Sasha as a lunch buddy with Miko, who has just started this week. She knows that Sasha will help Miko feel like she is a part of things right from the start.

## Feisty

The feisty or active temperament type is the one that can hold many challenges for providers. This cluster of traits includes the following:

- A higher level of activity, which may mean a child moves from center to center without finishing a job

- High distractibility and low persistence, which also points to behaviors that might be frustrating for a teacher if a child doesn't complete tasks or stay in place long enough to learn that activity

- Interference with the play or learning of other children when a child is bored or wants to keep moving

- High intensity, which makes everything the child does louder and bigger

On a positive note, a child who is feisty and active brings a lot of energy and zest to the program, with never a dull moment!

> Nicholas comes into the center each morning at full speed ahead, and his teachers don't think he ever slows down! It's hard to get him to stay at a table activity for longer than five minutes, and group time is a constant battle of interruptions. Some of the boys get caught up in his energy at times, but often the children want to avoid him because of the disruption he spreads.

## Fearful

The slow-to-warm-up or fearful temperament type can present some challenging behaviors as well. Temperament traits in this type can include the following:

- High levels of withdrawing behaviors, including not wanting to participate in a new activity, game, or program or with new children or teachers

- Lower levels of adaptability, which can mean a child takes longer to feel comfortable with new people

- Using aggression or similar challenging behaviors when asked by a peer to share a preferred activity instead of moving on to the next activity

- Not wanting to transition to a new activity or go on a field trip since it is not part of the routine or regular schedule

- Refusing to participate and having tantrums to avoid a change

On the positive side, a slow-to-warm child may be more reflective and observant, watching before she acts. She can be a stabilizing force in the program for those children who tend to move before they think.

> Ruby loves to be in the reading nook and the art center, but Teacher says she has to go to outside play. Ruby does not like outside play because it is too loud and she doesn't like the way the ground crackles under her feet.

## Understanding Your Own Temperament

It is important for teachers to have an understanding of their own temperament traits and how they perceive their dominant-traits cluster. All of us react to others, including children, with a set of behaviors that have been piloted by our temperaments. For instance, if you tend to be high in adaptability, you will be able to manage your classroom when a coteacher calls in sick. You don't see obstacles as much as you see solutions. However, if you tend to cluster more in the feisty range with a more negative mood and less adaptability, crying that escalates into a tantrum may make you feel like finding a new job! When you know that your temperament can influence how you feel or how you will react, you can take a breath and recoup before you take action.

### Using a Temperament Sorter

A temperament sorter is a way to identify temperament using a scale from high to low. It has been widely used by child developmentalists for many years to determine a child's temperament traits and clusters of traits. It is also helpful for adults to take the sorter to see where they fall in comparison to a child they are rating. Look again at the nine temperament traits and the range from low to high. Consider the following temperament sorter with your own personality instead of a child in mind. Jot down where you think you fall along each of the nine traits.

### Activity Level

How active is the child from an early age? Does she tend to be very busy most of the time, or does she tend toward quiet activities?

**Low Impact**          **Midrange**          **High Impact**

1    2    3    4    5    6    7    8    9    10

### Distractibility

How well does she pay attention if not particularly interested? Can her attention be diverted easily, or does she stay concentrated on a task?

**Low Impact**          **Midrange**          **High Impact**

1    2    3    4    5    6    7    8    9    10

### Persistence

Does the child stay with something she doesn't really like to do? If it becomes difficult, does she stay with it or move to the next game?

**Low Impact**          **Midrange**          **High Impact**

1    2    3    4    5    6    7    8    9    10

### Adaptability

How does the child deal with transitions or changes in routine? Does she roll with it or make a fuss when it is time to move to a new activity?

**Low Impact**          **Midrange**          **High Impact**

1    2    3    4    5    6    7    8    9    10

### Approach/Withdrawal

What is the child's initial response to newness? What is her reaction to new foods, places, activities, people, and clothes? Does she eagerly approach a new friend or tend toward hesitancy about new people?

| Low Impact | | | | Midrange | | | | High Impact | |
| --- | --- | --- | --- | --- | --- | --- | --- | --- | --- |
| 1 | 2 | 3 | 4 | 5 | 6 | 7 | 8 | 9 | 10 |

### Intensity

How loud is the child, whether happy or unhappy? How much energy does she use to express joy, anger, and frustration?

| Low Impact | | | | Midrange | | | | High Impact | |
| --- | --- | --- | --- | --- | --- | --- | --- | --- | --- |
| 1 | 2 | 3 | 4 | 5 | 6 | 7 | 8 | 9 | 10 |

### Regularity

How predictable is the child in her patterns of sleep, appetite, or bodily functions? Does she usually sleep at the same time, or is her napping time all over the place and unpredictable?

| Low Impact | | | | Midrange | | | | High Impact | |
| --- | --- | --- | --- | --- | --- | --- | --- | --- | --- |
| 1 | 2 | 3 | 4 | 5 | 6 | 7 | 8 | 9 | 10 |

### Sensory Threshold

How does the child react to sensory stimulation: noise, light, colors, smells, pain, tastes, textures in clothing and food? Is she overstimulated or bothered by different sensations? Or does she show little reaction to sensory stimulation like a loud noise?

| Low Impact | | | | Midrange | | | | High Impact | |
| --- | --- | --- | --- | --- | --- | --- | --- | --- | --- |
| 1 | 2 | 3 | 4 | 5 | 6 | 7 | 8 | 9 | 10 |

### Mood

What is the child's predominant mood? Is she generally more negative or positive?

| Low Impact | | | | Midrange | | | | High Impact | |
| --- | --- | --- | --- | --- | --- | --- | --- | --- | --- |
| 1 | 2 | 3 | 4 | 5 | 6 | 7 | 8 | 9 | 10 |

Once you have completed the temperament sorter, look for any pattern that may have emerged. Try to identify your dominant temperament traits. If you marked several traits in the midrange, or with a combination of high adaptability, approach, and positive mood, you are probably flexible in your temperament type. If you see yourself as low on adaptability and persistence, high on activity level and intensity, your temperament type is closer to feisty. If you see yourself as low on approach and adaptability and negative in mood, your temperament type may be fearful.

## Why Your Temperament Matters

Understanding your own temperament traits and style is important for many reasons as you work with young children. For one thing, when you have the same dominant temperament trait as a child in your program, you may find that your similarities can cause clashes between the two of you. You might wonder why you are struggling so much with a child with whom you have so much in common. Think about your dominant traits. If you both have high persistence, that goes well when you are both working together to finish a task or he is your helper of the week and wants to make sure the bulletin board is perfect. But it can cause conflict on the days when you need "just good enough" on an art project because there is a fire drill in ten minutes and this child isn't ready to put the paints away.

Conversely, having different temperament traits can also cause conflict between you and a child with whom you are working. It is easy to see why different temperament traits could clash. A child with high intensity will feel more strongly and express more loudly than someone in the midrange. If an adult caring for the child has low intensity, it may seem like every reaction is a nuclear meltdown! Walking sounds like marching, singing sounds like screeching, and even screams of joy are hard to distinguish from screams of pain. On the other hand, if the teacher has high intensity and has big reactions to what is going on around him, a child with low intensity may be overwhelmed by the "bigness" of his sounds and actions.

A classroom will always be made up of a mixture of temperaments. Knowing your own style of relating will help you connect to a variety of differences in others, especially in the diversity of children you will serve. You will rarely have a program of all flexible personalities! As you embrace differences, you affirm children for authentically being who they are.

## Relationships and Temperament

As we consider children and the diversity of temperament styles they bring to our programs, it helps to reflect on our own dispositions to understand why we feel the way we do about children's behaviors. Your own temperament and particularly your dominant disposition traits have had an influence on the choices you have made and the relationships you have with others in your life, professionally and personally. You may remember how, from an early age, your personality affected the way you learned in school or made friends in your neighborhood. Take a moment to consider some of the main ways in which you may have identified yourself throughout your life:

- Did you see yourself as active, shy, stubborn, resistant to change, or eager to try new things?

- Did others use some of these words when they referred to you? Were you ever labeled by an adult as hyper, hard to handle, or "an Eeyore"?

- Did you ever feel that some of your basic dispositions were at odds with your siblings or teachers at school?

Here is a personal example that I experienced growing up with high activity and high distractibility temperament traits:

> In my own early school years, I spent many days with my desk pushed into the corner of the classroom or out in the hallway because I moved too much and I had a tendency to talk when I wasn't supposed to. I was highly active, so I seemed to get into a lot of trouble, getting up when I needed to be seated and so on. In the third grade, though, I had a teacher who for some reason made me the "teacher's pet," something I had never experienced. She honored my natural need to move by giving me tasks that kept my hands and mind busy. She didn't punish me for my dominant temperament trait but found ways to adapt the environment to help me be successful. I am still an active, highly distractible person, but I have found ways to make it work for me as a successful adult.

You have a unique personality that has influenced the many decisions you have made over your lifetime. You have learned over time to make adaptations and adjustments in order to be successful in your world. For example, if you have a high activity level, you may have found ways to incorporate movement into your day rather than sit at a desk. Or maybe you have chosen a career that lets you use your activity level during the course of your work. If you have high impulsivity, you may be in a position that lets you change directions throughout the day or creatively present the same activity in new ways.

In making adaptations to the way you react to the world around you, you were probably more successful if you had supportive adults like my third-grade teacher. Through the eyes of a caring and responsive adult, you learned that you were uniquely made and were celebrated for your personality. You also know that, unfortunately, this is not always the case. At other times, you may have been told you were naughty or wrong because of who you naturally were. Some adults may have tried to squelch your natural wiring because it didn't fit their idea of a quiet child or the environment you were in. A child with high intensity can be taught skills so that when she walks it is less like marching in a parade, but she will not become someone who can sneak up on others! The goal is to help her learn and practice some quieter methods of walking when softer steps are important, knowing that her quiet is going to be different from a child who does not have high intensity.

As you consider your life and all that has occurred because of your own temperament traits and disposition, it can be the lens through which you see the children you work with and the behaviors they exhibit that challenge you at times. When we look at each child we work with, we know that all of them come to us with the same nine temperament traits that we have, on a range from high to low to somewhere in between. Some will be flexible and easy, some will be more withdrawn and fearful, and some will be active and feisty. At any given time, challenging behaviors can erupt because children are learning and practicing how to navigate complicated social worlds in child care and preschool. Children are also reacting to one another's temperament traits that are sometimes at odds with their own.

Our goal is not to fundamentally change a child or require changes that go against his basic nature. Instead, we want to offer an environment and instructions that create an atmosphere that guides positive behaviors and interactions as children gain new skills. As Berk (2013) points out,

> What is important is that babies respond differently to similar circumstances. These personal behavior patterns appear to persist into childhood, affecting how others respond. Parents and caregivers play a role in the persistence of personality traits. One caregiver might regard a child as distractible, impulsive, and hard to manage while another might perceive the same child as [an] eager, active, happy-go-lucky runabout (391).

Our commitment to children needs to include a greater understanding and empathy surrounding how they each react to the world around them as we help them in their interactions with peers and with us, knowing we all have different personalities and styles of interacting. When we honor a child's unique personality, we set the stage for positive social-emotional development as he sees himself as worthy and his peers as valued.

## Influences of Environment on Temperament

Chapters 3 through 11 will include strategies early educators can implement that will help in including children with each dominant temperament trait. These strategies include environmental and programmatic adaptations. It is worth noting again that temperament is environmentally influenced as well as genetically set. The degree to which temperament is both natural and environmental is hard to measure, particularly because temperament can modify somewhat in some children as they grow. For instance, a child who is hard to soothe as an infant (negative mood, low regulation) may develop better regulatory skills that help her become a less fussy child later on. A child low on regulation will not become highly regulated, however. Research from Berk (2013) indicates that "the overall stability of temperament is low in infancy and toddlerhood and only moderate from the preschool years," though evidence also shows that many children will remain the same temperamentally (423). Another example of how the environment can influence a child's natural inclinations to act a certain way would be in his familiarity with a setting. A child might be quiet and subdued in the first days of a new child care setting even though her parents say she is full of energy at home. This doesn't mean that the child's temperament has changed; her true energy expressions will come out when she is comfortable enough to be herself. For instance, most children can keep their need to move in check for a certain period of time, but a child with a high activity level will eventually release that energy. The good news is that we can help children learn to regulate impulses that come into conflict with the setting they are in. We will examine the influence of the environment on temperament, including guidance practices, in chapter 2.

The environment can work as one of your primary tools to regulate and, to some degree, adjust children's reactions related to temperament traits so each of them can be successful in different sorts of settings. No one child should ever be expected to behave exactly like another because of the environment, but you can help each child manage some of the ups and downs that might be related to a temperament trait through environment supports. The environment for early educators includes

- the classroom;

- the family child care program in a home setting;

- individual activity centers;

- outside play area;

- kitchen and eating areas;

- nurse's office;

- bathroom space; and

- areas used for taking a break or other quiet spaces.

This is good news for the early childhood educator because it means the child care setting can be organized in ways that enhance natural temperament traits and also prevent some of the challenging behaviors that may go along with some temperament traits.

## Organizing the Classroom to Fit Different Temperaments

Your classroom can be your first and best tool for preventing challenging behaviors before they happen. The environment can be set up in ways that help a child stay focused or use his energy in positive ways. For instance, open areas can be changed into smaller activity centers with natural barriers like bookshelves that prevent an overenergized child from running. A child who is sensitive to a lot of noise can benefit from having the quiet centers grouped near each other and the louder activity areas set together in another area of the center. Being aware of how much sensory stimulation is in the room (smell, noise, wall decorations, and so forth) and working to decrease it can help a child who has high distractibility stay focused longer.

Effective classroom organization would include a space for a child who feels overwhelmed or overstimulated to go for a break. It is up to you to make the rules for this space and how it is used and what you might include in it (books, pillows, some toys or not). A take-a-break space or quiet nook helps a child with low adaptability or low regularity learn to know his own body and exercise impulse control. Your space is now your best intervention strategy before behaviors even occur!

## Choosing Programming to Fit Different Temperaments

Your child care programming is the other area of your environment that you can organize proactively to prevent challenging behaviors. You can accomplish this through intentionally planning for children with diverse temperament types. For instance, when your programming and policies ensure that all children are consistently immersed in learning experiences that are developmentally appropriate and high quality, as well as connected to responsive caregivers who understand their needs, children will feel safe and less apt to act out. They understand that their needs will be met. Challenging behaviors may still occur, but children who trust their caregiver and feel secure in their environment can use more of their energy on regulating themselves and developing social skills. For instance, a consistent schedule that is referred to throughout the day by the teacher builds internal regulation for all children and especially for a child who has less regulation. Programs that are disorganized and without routines will increase anxiousness in a child who already has trouble with low adaptability and low regulation, resulting in a child who refuses to move to a new activity or throws a tantrum to stay put.

You cannot control how a child has been genetically wired, a gift from her parents or grandparents, but you are able to control the classroom or family child care environment to a large degree. You can make accommodations to lighting, sound, the daily schedule, and many other features that naturally support a child's dominant traits. This is important in helping prevent or extinguish a challenging behavior before it ever happens.

Temperament is part of who a child is, naturally. Again, Berk (2013) points out that "[evidence] . . . confirms that experience can modify biologically based temperament traits considerably, although children rarely change from one extreme to another—that is, a shy preschooler practically never becomes highly sociable, and irritable children seldom become easy-going" (423). As early educators, we want to help children be the best they can be in their developmental outcomes and in social-emotional development. We want to embrace a child's unique nature and build on those strengths. This book is intended to support you with practical strategies for doing just that.

Jessica and Ivan are in the three-year-old class. They are best friends. Jessica is the first to try anything and welcomes new activities as well as new children at Busy Bees Preschool. Ivan is more reluctant to try something new until Jessica has first, but then he will join in. Jessica will show him how to do something if he has never done it before. He doesn't mind when she runs off to play with someone new because he likes to sit in the reading nook and finish his favorite book. Together they make a great team!

# 2

# Guiding through Each Child's Strengths

Children come to our programs with a wiring unique to their own genetics and the environment in which they have been raised. Early educators want to honor each child as an individual while also helping them be as successful as they can be.

In this chapter, we will look at the ways you can support the unique personality of each child as you offer guidance to navigate the social and emotional world that children are immersed in, particularly in child care. Guidance will be your foundation on which the strategies in the next chapters build. If this were a pyramid, guidance would be the bottom, where environment and relationships support each child naturally without specific interventions.

## What Is Meant by *Guidance*?

Dan Gartrell (2012) offers this definition of behavior guidance in the context of early childhood: "A way of teaching that nurtures each child's potential through consistently positive (sometimes firm, but always friendly) interactions; classroom management that teaches rather than punishes" (156). Learning to teach a child how to make a better choice, whether in responding to her friend or reacting to a strong emotion, is key here because her experience is limited, and she only knows what has worked for her up to this point.

As we consider children's behavior through the lens of temperament, we see that many of the actions or activities that are challenging to us in child care are a result of how a child reacts to and interacts with the world around her based on that limited experience of perhaps thirty-six or forty-eight months of life. For example, if adults frequently respond to a four-year-old by telling him that he is their hyper boy, he begins to see himself as somehow "wrong" because it is not said with pleasure or affection. He may not know what "hyper" is, but he knows from the tone and expressions on the faces of these adults that it is not something to feel good about. Still, he has all this energy inside of him churning around because his temperament is high in activity level. What is he supposed to do with it so he doesn't keep getting in trouble? This is where the teaching rather than punishing comes into play for the early childhood professional.

## Teaching vs. Punishing

When we show a child what we want them to do—for instance, "go get a teacher if someone is bullying you"—we are teaching them a skill. When we teach through guidance techniques, we prepare a child for the next time something happens. Punishment is very different from teaching through our guidance. Punishment often shames a child but doesn't teach him a replacement behavior. For example, let's say a child has high intensity and repeatedly runs into friends with bear hugs that knock them over. If we tell the boy he has to go to time-out because he doesn't know how to be a good friend, he is embarrassed and still doesn't know how to approach his friends well. Time-out often serves as a punishment because it doesn't teach a new replacement behavior. In this example, a teacher could say to the child, "Oops, your friend got knocked over. Let's make sure she is okay. Then let's practice asking if we can hug first. How does that feel?" Now he has a new skill to use in his social relationships.

Research tells us that punishment tends to make children feel bad about themselves rather than reflect on the behavior they exhibited. Children who have some particular temperament traits like high intensity or high activity levels need to be taught behaviors that won't put them at odds with the rules or hurt their relationships with other children. For instance, they can take a break and jump on the mini-trampoline when they feel lots of energy inside instead of running down the hallway. If a child is put into a time-out because he broke the rule against running inside, he still doesn't know what to do with all that energy inside of him and will likely run again when he needs to release it, unless we have shown him other ways to use it. The four-year-old boy in the example above needs a caring and responsive adult to guide him in regulating his energy so he can learn what is appropriate *inside* the classroom, for instance at circle time or in the lunchroom, and what is appropriate *outside*, like when he is standing in line or playing on the gym equipment. He may not be able to handle as much wait time as others, so he should be at the front of the line more often in transitions, and he may also need more frequent breaks to go jump on the mini-trampoline. His teacher is the one who can guide him with those positive interactions in order to nurture his potential, as Gartrell (2012) points out to us. We can turn around the negative language and attitudes that children have experienced and show them the positive characteristics of their innate personalities.

### Pitfalls of Labeling

Looking again at the four-year-old boy with high energy in the example above, when he begins to see himself as the negative label that teachers have given him, he also stops seeing the potential that he has to be successful in other ways. When a teacher frequently refers to a child in her care as "my crabby apple," that little girl knows there is something about that name that isn't making the teacher happy. If other staff nod and laugh, it is reinforced that there may be something wrong with her, even though she doesn't know for sure what that is. A child who tends toward negative on the mood trait is not as cheerful as the child who is more positive in mood, but there is not a value attached to temperament traits. Children simply are who they are, and the early childhood provider's role is to create environments that support learning and relationship building for every child. Labels create barriers to that goal.

That same little boy with high energy is just the boy you need when you want to get everyone excited about a field trip or to help move equipment around outside. The little girl who is more reticent about new ideas informs us with a different viewpoint on the activities we are planning. When we treat temperament traits as special gifts, we allow children to feel good about who they are innately, and we give them permission to be all they can be.

## Knowing Each Child as an Individual

In order to know how to best respond with positive interactions to each child in a child care program, you need to be familiar with the individual temperament traits of the children you care for. Consider the following when determining how to respond to a child:

- How will you assess and record a child's temperament traits?

- What are the dominant traits that every child expresses in your child care?

- Where does each child fall on a temperament cluster or type?

- How does your own temperament match up or conflict with the different children in your care?

From there, you can offer tailor-made guidance strategies using your environment, your child-adult interactions, and your activities, creating programming specific to that child's needs. Not only is this a positive approach, but it can prevent some challenging behaviors from happening in the first place.

## Avoiding Expulsion and Suspension

The consequences for children who do not get individualized guidance is often expulsion or suspension from their child care program. *Expulsion* is the removal or dismissal of a child from an early care and education program, generally due to issues related to challenging behaviors. Other words or phrases used for expulsion can include these:

- He was disenrolled.

- The family was asked to leave.

- It wasn't a good fit.

- The parents chose to go elsewhere.

- Staff were frustrated and wouldn't work with the child.

- Other parents complained too much.

*Suspension* is the temporary removal of a child from the child care setting for any period of time. It frequently means the parent or caregiver has been called to come and pick up the child for the day or for the rest of the week, often a precursor to expulsion. Some suspensions are on-site suspensions, like the child being sent to the director's office. The research on preschool expulsion is alarming because of the number of children who are expelled from early childhood programs and the impact it has on their ongoing social-emotional development.

Nationally, preschool children are over three times more likely to be expelled from their state prekindergarten programs when compared with children in kindergarten through grade twelve. In addition, a report by Walter S. Gilliam and colleagues at the Yale Child Study Center (2016) found that

> Black preschoolers are 3.6 times as likely to receive one or more suspensions relative to White preschoolers. This is particularly concerning as Black children make up only 19% of preschool enrollment, but comprise 47% of preschoolers suspended one or more times. Similarly, boys are three times as likely as girls to be suspended one or more times.

Part of the reason for this high expulsion rate, according to the *Policy Statement on Expulsion and Suspension Policies in Early Childhood Settings* (HHS, and ED 2014), is that some children's behavior is inappropriately labeled as challenging when in fact the behaviors may be appropriate to the child's age and developmental stage. In addition, research by Walter S. Gilliam and his colleagues at the Yale Child Study Center (2016) revealed that implicit bias by teachers toward Black students might account for higher expulsion rates. Implicit bias is any unconsciously held set of attributes or associations you might give to a social group—in this case, children of color. It can influence how a teacher perceives a behavior from a child and also what kind of guidance they use for a behavior. Expulsion appears to be used more frequency when a child is Black. The consequences of expulsion for all children are negative. Children who are expelled are left with a feeling of failure and loss of peer relationships as well as any attached relationships with primary caregivers. This loss can damage ongoing social-emotional development and harm future relationship building.

Early childhood teachers need support and training so they can understand why a child is demonstrating a particular behavior. Only in learning skills can teachers provide the guidance a child needs to learn a more appropriate behavior. For example, if a child wanders from activity center to activity center and only briefly takes part with any interest, she may be seen as a girl who bothers everyone else, who isn't a good learner, and who can't pay attention. She may get a label like "my busybody." The label doesn't guide or teach the child. With the right support to the child, though, the provider might learn that she will stay engaged longer if the teacher provides positive reinforcement and specific encouragement when she is successful. To help her be successful, the teacher might start the child in her preferred activities (the block area) where she can experience success before expecting her to go to less preferred tasks (sitting for story time).

Expelling her because she is a distraction to other children and requires more teacher time to stay involved in an activity doesn't give her any new skills and only causes damage to her ongoing social-emotional development and sense of self-worth. She begins to see herself as not competent and not worthy of the teacher's goodwill. It is hard to reverse these negative messages that are internalized by children at a tender age. However, when we know a child's temperament traits and see them through a strength-based lens, we can use that knowledge to support her. The child who bounces from activity to activity can become a child who learns to regulate her impulsivity by staying five minutes longer, then seven minutes, then ten minutes until she is staying with her peers for the whole activity. She experiences success and sees herself as she sees her peers: capable.

Hazel is bright and intuitive at four years old. She is also highly social and very persistent. She tends to want to have things go according to her plan. Unfortunately, staff at Bright Stars Child Care see her as bossy and difficult to manage because of her strong personality. Hazel has decided that all the girls have to wear dresses every day or she won't play with them. The four other girls in her classroom are complying. Parents are complaining to staff because they don't want to send their daughters in dresses every day, but the girls are in tears in the morning because they are afraid that Hazel will exclude them. The teachers went to the director to say that they would like Hazel to be asked to leave the program because the parents are all upset. The director believes that, instead, they can work with Hazel's natural disposition to be in charge by giving her more responsibility in the classroom in a way that uses her skills. In addition, the director is going to institute "special wear days"—like pajama day, jeans day, and so on—for the next five days to break the dress-wearing habit.

## Building on Key Strengths

Building on a child's key strengths from his temperament can prevent challenging behaviors when you work *with* a child's natural tendencies instead of *against* them. When the environment and the guidance strategies used in the early childhood setting fit a child's temperament, it allows the child to thrive and flourish. It can actually cause more challenging reactions in children when we are pushing against or trying to squelch what is for that child a natural feeling. For instance, if a child naturally prefers consistency and routine and has trouble with changes in the schedule, it can throw him into great distress when we spring something on him the day of the event without any preparation. Even if what we have planned is a last-minute outing to the park across the street, if it is out of the ordinary and he was not prepped for it, he may become unglued by the change and the lack of time to get ready for it. If, on the other hand, we had started talking to him about it early in the day and asked him how he wanted to get ready for it, we could have helped him organize himself so it wasn't a complete surprise. Better yet is planning events in advance so children like this boy can talk about it for a few days ahead to get ready for it.

> Rollie has a small picture schedule he wears on his belt loop that shows him all the transitions in his school day. He looks at the pictures frequently when he is unsure of what is coming next, even though the schedule has been the same since he enrolled four weeks ago. He also has a special picture schedule for Friday because his class is going to the zoo. He has been practicing it for three days. It includes getting on the bus, going to the zoo, eating lunch at the zoo, and getting back on the bus to come back to his school. He is getting excited because he loves polar bears and lions.

In this example, Rollie is ready for a change in the schedule because his teacher has prepared him ahead of time and he knows exactly what to expect. His low adaptability and anxiety about change have been mitigated by the picture schedule that he will bring with him on Friday to refer to if he feels insecure. This clever teacher has avoided what could have been a major meltdown by Rollie on Friday morning when he had to get on the bus, disturbing all the other children and affecting Rollie in a negative way as well.

Looking at the positive side, when you know what a child's dominant temperament trait is, you can incorporate the strength of that trait into activities you are planning. For instance, a child with high intensity is just the right child to lead the whole group in marching exercises in the morning or to help motivate others who might be dragging their heels into getting a task accomplished. A child who is less adaptable can be the helper who goes through the visual picture schedule with the teacher in the morning. Ask the child who is overly sensitive to sounds to help you "soundproof" some of the quieter activity areas; you will be surprised at the creative ideas they may come up with.

It is easier to work with a child's natural temperament than to fight against it, trying to change something that is biologically wired within the child. You will not get a child who has high levels of withdrawal to be the class clown, but you can help that child feel safe and secure enough to approach a peer to ask her to play a board game together.

## Supporting Different Personality Types

The unique temperament that children bring to child care can be supported by the early childhood staff in ways that will ensure positive interactions rather than bringing out challenging behaviors. One way is by examining staff attitudes. First, we all need to think about the temperament traits we possess that we may feel negatively about because of personal life experiences. Once we are honest about our feelings, we can recognize how this affects our perceptions of others. It can influence the way we see the same disposition in a child we care for.

Staff need to understand temperament from a child development lens. We can teach early educators to recognize the natural wiring of a child so they are committed to building on strengths in order for the child to be most successful. A skilled early childhood professional knows how to adjust a schedule, activity, or event to accommodate a child who is overly active, disengaged, or fearful of change.

Early educators must be knowledgeable of developmentally appropriate practice because it informs us of how to make adaptations for learning needs regardless of a behavior. Developmentally appropriate practice will be discussed later in this chapter. When you are using this lens, you are looking at the whole child, including his ability, age, family system, culture, and temperament style. In addition, you will have program policies aligned with developmentally appropriate practice that support children and families through a philosophy of inclusion and acceptance. Even greater than a staff person's commitment to meeting unique learning needs is the overall program's commitment to supporting children as they are when they come to a program.

It is important to note here that in any child care program, change needs to be seen as constant because children are ever-changing. Successful programming for all types of temperaments are adaptable to a variety of situations and personalities.

## Understanding the Function of Behavior

Using temperament as your lens when examining challenging behaviors in your child care program can help you understand where a child is coming from when she reacts a particular way to environmental influences. Temperament gives you an awareness of what she may need to be successful in your program. But what can be difficult to understand is why one child with high intensity reacts without challenging behaviors and another child is aggressive when she doesn't get what she wants.

The function of the behavior is the "why" of the behavior. A child may have high intensity as a dominant temperament trait, and you understand that this trait impacts her reactions to the world around her. What you may not understand is why she uses a particular behavior that puts her at odds with you or other children. When we narrow behaviors down to what a child is trying to tell us, her behavior is usually serving one of the following purposes:

- **To escape:** a child is seeking to avoid something that is unpleasant or undesirable to her

- **To obtain:** a child wants to get attention, a preferred item or activity, or sensory stimulation

### To Escape

Escaping or getting away behaviors are used when a child needs to avoid or leave a situation or other child who is challenging to him in some way. If his temperament is low on intensity, he may find a child higher on intensity as very disruptive to his play. He may begin to use a behavior, like biting, to get the other child away from him. If biting works and the child cries and is picked up and taken to another part of the room, then his behavior is reinforced by the adult and the child. He is likely to use it again because it worked for him.

### To Obtain

Obtaining behaviors are when a child wants or needs something and works on getting it. It becomes a challenging behavior when it is at odds with your rules or other children's wants or needs, or it causes harm to the child or his peers. For example, a child who has high sensory awareness may use a behavior like crying or whining to get more time to play outside because her proprioceptive system needs muscle input. If whining is a behavior that usually gets her what she needs, she will continue to use whining.

# Broad Strategies of Guidance Approaches to Children's Behaviors

There are fundamental daily practices that early educators can use to support the personality differences of all the children they work with. The approach and outlook that you bring to your programs every day impacts the attitudes and reactions of the children with whom you are working.

## Tone and Words

Your interactions with children include the tone you use when you speak to them and the choice of words you use. The way you talk to children affects how they feel about themselves, which in turn affects how they react to you and others. For example, a child who hears, "You are a good problem solver," begins to believe in his value to the child care community and wants to be a positive problem solver. We have dozens of opportunities throughout the day to give children positive affirmations. When your tone must be firm, as in, "Rebecca, remember, kind words," it can also be respectful. We set the stage for positive behaviors with our language.

## Body Language

Your body language is an intentional way that you can support children positively before any challenging behaviors occur. We can reinforce positive behaviors by giving lots of smiles and affirmations when a child is doing exactly what we had hoped she would be doing. For example, if a typically fidgety child is sitting somewhat still in circle time, a smile and encouraging look tells her she is doing a good thing right then. We often save our "looks" for disapproval, but when we think to reverse this approach, we are adding one more encouragement to a child to use positive behaviors.

## Your Reactions

Interactions with children go on throughout your whole day. You can affirm a child's natural temperament through the way you respond and react to his reactions. Once again, a positive reaction on the part of the teacher can go far in helping a child see himself as valued and competent. Your reaction, joined with your words and body language, give messages to children about your acceptance of them.

### Show Acceptance

When you show nurturance and responsiveness to a child, you build a sense of value for that child. A child who feels accepted is a child who is going to be more positive in his interactions with peers and adults because he doesn't have to prove he is worthy.

> Kwan's first few days at her new child care center were very hard for her because everyone started in free choice, meaning they could go to any activity center they wanted to, but she wasn't sure what to do and she didn't have any friends yet. She just moved from center to center and felt very lonely. On the fourth day, her teacher met her at the door and said, "If you want a hug, you can hug me until you are ready to start play." Kwan hugged her teacher for a long time that day, and when she felt safe she went to the block space. The next day, her teacher greeted her again, but this time she only needed a short hug and she was off to play. Soon she didn't need the hug at all. Kwan's teacher gave her a sense of security until she was ready to take off on her own.

In addition, consider all the various types of supports you give to children during the child care day that are part of your regular practice. These are embedded strategies that offer children positive guidance and tell them important messages about who they are and what they can achieve. Sometimes these supports are intuitive as you watch a child off to the side who is not engaged. Sometimes the supports are intentional practice to ensure all children are included. For example, you can intentionally provide words to the child who is struggling with play skills but wants to enter play with a group of peers. You can cue some of the children with a predetermined sign, like a red circle on a piece of paper, when a transition is coming up, because you know they need an extra five minutes for cleanup. As part of your ongoing and intentional practice, you allow for more child-directed than teacher-directed activities because you know children gain more from leading their own play, so they have more time in dramatic play than a craft activity. Finally, you provide ongoing physical and emotional support to all the little and big ouches that children encounter each day when feelings get hurt or someone falls off the slide. In all these ways, children learn that being busy or quiet isn't "bad" and that they are okay just the way they are.

## Changing Difficult Behaviors

To change a child's behavior from challenging to more acceptable, helping them make friends and learn successfully, you will need to do a few things. Looking back to our earlier definition of guidance as "teaching that nurtures each child's potential through consistently positive . . . interactions" (Gartrell 2012, 156), what you do each day with children comprises the guidance you are providing them. As we have seen, guidance can both be part of overall program practice and be specific to one child's needs. You can use strategies for guiding explicit behaviors that are manifested because of a child's dominant temperament traits, helping a child achieve positive outcomes. At the same time, your program can be set up in such a way that it serves as an ongoing behavior strategy with responsive caregiving, sensory awareness, and consistent routines. Some of what you are doing each day for every child is already built into your environmental supports; some of what you are doing each day for every child is interventions built around their temperament needs.

## Know Each Child's Temperament

Knowing each child's dominant temperament traits will give you context for determining what a behavior might be related to. Temperament influences behaviors even when the function of the behavior is not directly related to the temperament trait. For instance, if a child is acting-out because she is tired from not getting sleep the night before, her acting out behaviors will be magnified if she already has a low adaptability and low flexibility.

Remember that it takes time to diminish the challenging parts of a behavior, so allow for a few weeks of consistent intervention using the strategies from this book to see changes. If the child has several temperament traits that cluster as feisty or fearful, combine strategies in those temperament traits. Remember, too, that she is doing the best she can with what she knows works for her. She needs adults to teach her new behaviors through guidance strategies.

## Use Observation

Use observation tools to find the function of a behavior that is persistently challenging. You can create a chart that tracks the time of day the behavior happens and what activity the child is engaged in. Then add what happens right before the behavior (the antecedent) and what happens immediately after the behavior (the consequence). Typically after a few days, a pattern emerges about the behavior. For example, a child who has never bitten others before has started biting peers. On the surface, it seems to be random and baffling. Once you begin to track the biting behaviors, though, you see that Alfonzo bites early in the day, usually before the first snack is offered. When the biting happens, he is almost always whisked away by a staff person to another part of the room and separated from peers (consequence). In this example, you might learn that Alfonzo needs a snack earlier to help prevent frustration caused by hunger. Alfonzo is not well regulated biologically, and until recently he always had a snack in the car on the way to child care. His routine changed when his dad began dropping him off.

### Intervene to Break the Pattern

Once you see a pattern, you can intervene and break the pattern. For instance, if you discover that a child has begun hitting after playing in large-group play in the early afternoon, you may determine the child is tired and needs an earlier nap than the schedule has allowed. If you know his temperament trait is low on regularity, you may not have realized when he was sleepy before because his napping seemed irregular. In the example above, giving a snack a bit earlier to a child who cannot wait until snacktime could prevent a challenging behavior from occurring.

## Tailoring Teaching Strategies for Temperament Styles

The following chapters will be more specific in outlining strategies for each of the nine temperament traits, but as an overall approach, guidance strategies can be embedded into the early childhood program to benefit all children regardless of temperament. Your goal, besides honoring each child's unique temperament, should be to prevent challenging behavior before it has a chance to occur! This is the purpose of guidance as part of overall program delivery in the way the environment is set up, interactions are built, staff are prepared, and programming is offered.

Practically, how is this accomplished? For one thing, early childhood professionals need to have knowledge in evidence-based guidance practices, meaning that the strategies you are using are supported by research and by what you have seen to be effective. You find these guidance practices in quality training and literature that has research to back it up. One example of quality training and resources is the pyramid model of behavior intervention found in the Technical Assistance Center on Social Emotional Intervention (TACSEI), a federally funded program that promotes positive social-emotional development. Free teaching tools are available to help teachers with practical strategies around behaviors. In addition, websites like the Center for Inclusive Child Care (www.inclusivechildcare.org) offer free courses on guidance and behavior strategies for early educators. Teachers need to have a network of resource support so that behaviors can be managed early, before they become problematic.

### Developmentally Appropriate Practice

Another important consideration in tailoring specific strategies to a child's temperament style is a program's philosophy about guidance as it relates to developmentally appropriate practice, or DAP. Developmentally appropriate practice is generally known by early childhood professionals as the framework by which teachers adapt programming and activities to meet the individual learning needs of all children. According to the National Association for the Education of Young Children (NAEYC), "DAP involves teachers meeting young children where they are, both as individuals and as part of a group; and helping each child meet challenging and achievable learning goals" (NAEYC, accessed 2020).

Developmentally appropriate practice can be used as a gauge for guidance in several ways. It includes the following:

- how a program supports staff interactions with children

- how it supports relationship building between children and peers as well as children and staff

- how it provides responsive, nurturing caregiving to all children

It means that early educators look at the chronological as well as developmental age of a child, his family system, and his cultural influences to meet his ongoing developmental needs. Temperament is part of the picture of the whole child. When designing guidance approaches, we need to consider the age and stage of the child. A child who is poorly regulated at age two will look and act differently than a child with regulation issues at age four. Our expectations about a child's emotional regulation will also differ based on how high or low we understand his levels of the regularity temperament trait to be.

Along with DAP is the assumption that staff will have age-appropriate expectations for children's behavior. As noted earlier in the policy statement on expulsion, inappropriate expectations may be one reason that children are expelled from programs at such a high rate. In my work at the Center for Inclusive Child Care, I see coaches trained in Relationship-Based Professional Development (RBPD) go into child care programs to work with staff, often because of behavior challenges. The challenges run a gamut of issues across ages and gender, from toddlers to older preschoolers. However, I frequently see teachers asking for help with older preschool boys. It's possible that the expectations some program staff hold for four-year-olds is not developmentally appropriate. These boys are bigger in size and have more language skills than their three-year-old friends. But they still are very inexperienced, with only forty-eight months of life in which to learn self-regulation, negotiation, problem-solving, and sometimes play and social competencies. Teachers may be expecting behaviors that are more sophisticated than what is realistic for the child they are working with. It's also worth noting that developmentally not all four-year-olds have mastered the same social-emotional milestones. A child who has had low persistence as a dominant trait may not have learned the same skills as some of his same-aged peers if he did not stick with all the learning tasks he was given in preschool. Knowing the child individually helps us tailor our guidance to his specific needs.

## Environmental and Programmatic Supports

Your physical environment involves many things. It is in the play areas, activity centers, eating area, outside space, and anywhere else in your physical structure that programming takes place. That gives you a lot to work with! Your physical environment is key to preventing many of the challenging behaviors that can happen when a child reacts to the world around him.

Supports for children's positive behavior can be built into the environment to help prevent challenging behaviors related to a child's temperament needs. Using the environment as a preventative tool is the philosophy behind several pyramid models of behavior guidance. To begin with, the way a program is physically laid out can encourage more positive behaviors. For instance, if space is set up with lots of natural boundaries like bookshelves that divide up activity centers, there is less open space for a highly active child to run or try to wrestle with a friend. This is a fairly easy change to make to the space. The general layout of a program can allow for quiet spaces like art and reading to be near each other and noisier areas like dramatic play and large-muscle activities to be closer to each other, giving children opportunities to stay active or to transition slowly in a quieter mode if they need to. They also aren't interrupting others.

A child who has a low threshold for noise may choose to spend more time in the quieter spaces of the center. When she has been in dramatic play for a while and feels she is getting overstimulated, she knows there is a quiet take-a-break space for her closer to the reading nook. In this way, she is supporting her own biological regulatory system with her own tools that you have made an every-day part of the program. You don't have to offer an intervention strategy for a child who uses a tantrum to leave a noisy group time; your environment is the intervention.

All children, whether high or low on a particular temperament trait, benefit from a consistent routine and visual supports. A picture schedule that you refer to multiple times during your day reinforces regulation and helps children build impulse-control skills. A take-a-break space also builds regulatory skills by giving a child a place to go and calm herself. These are two easy adaptations to your program that support every child but especially those who struggle with change and regulation, with traits like low adaptability, low persistence, low regularity, and high sensory awareness.

Ongoing environmental and programmatic accommodations are part of a high-quality early childhood setting. Whether there are eight children or thirty, the environment is never static. It is important to be constantly assessing the physical environment and making changes as needed for each child. A wise teacher once told me never to move your furniture around on the weekend and surprise the children (and staff!) on Monday morning unless you want to see a lot of challenging behaviors!

Children who need consistency and tend toward anxiousness will have great difficulty adapting to new surroundings that they had no warning about. Keep major changes to a minimum unless the child who has low adapting skills has had prep time to get ready for changes and perhaps even helps with the moves.

Assessing your physical environment can be formally accomplished with a tool like an Environmental Ratings Scale, or you may simply keep track of where a child's challenging behaviors tend to occur and make adaptations to that area. Scatterplots are easy tools to mark where and when a challenging behavior occurred.

Here is a list of some areas you can add to or adjust in the physical environment that will help support positive behaviors for children with different temperament needs.

- **Visual supports:** Visual supports include picture schedules, posted rules, cue cards, signage, and any other visual tool that helps a child build regulatory skills as well as feel safe and secure. It can also include printed labels on clear containers that make it easy to clean up or choose materials. Any visual support should include the printed word for the object along with a picture of the object.

- **Transitions:** For many children with temperament traits that make change more difficult, cutting back on transitions is key. In addition, spending the extra time to ensure that children who struggle with change have a clear understanding of what is going to happen next will allow them to best prepare themselves. It could be a visual support like a personal picture schedule or an auditory cue that everyone recognizes as the cleanup song. Consistency is critical to the success of an auditory cue.

- **Group times:** These can be especially difficult for a child who is high in activity and energy and doesn't like to sit for long or for a child with high distractibility who has difficulty with engagement. Specific strategies for each temperament will be discussed in coming chapters, but there are several ways to adapt your group time to help children who have trouble sitting. First consider adapting the length of time a child needs to sit before they can move out of the circle. You can use a timer that is extended gradually, building up the length of time he can stay seated. Make sure you are using comfortable seating. Many children have difficulty with the crisscross-applesauce style of sitting. It can give some children a sense of loss of balance, which prevents them from tuning in to your story or messages. Rather than requiring children to cross their legs, consider instead letting them lie on their stomachs, which centers them and helps them pay better attention. Another idea that can work for children who fidget or want to touch others is using individual rugs that represent a boundary between children.

- **Gross-muscle play:** Children with high activity levels may need to get sensory input into their proprioceptive or muscle sense with play that uses their trunks, arms, and legs. Some children may need to be the first in line to get outside to play in order to get the most muscle and joint input. Let them lead a parade around the classroom where they are allowed to march as loud as they can. Mini-trampolines, where allowed by licensing regulations, are a great way to relieve excess energy.

- **Quiet space/time:** A child who is slow to warm up or has a low sensory threshold for sounds can benefit from opportunities to take a break and regroup his sensory system. Designating spaces for children to retreat to for some quiet time can prevent a child from becoming distressed from too much stimulation. This can prevent behaviors like crying, biting, or withdrawing from others. The purpose of the quiet space needs to be explained to your group, and they may need to practice using it for a while. You might post one or two simple rules on how you want to see it used—whether a child can take a book with him, for instance. It can be as simple as a group of pillows in one corner or an actual space that is more removed from the action but still within your observation.

## Emotional Accommodations

The emotional environment you create is as important as the physical environment for promoting children's natural dispositions with positive guidance approaches. This can include the following elements:

- **Respect:** All children feel honored and respected by the early childhood professionals in your program. No child is singled out with a label like "my overactive one" or "my nervous child." Staff seek ways to promote the natural tendencies of children in the program through positive praise and encouragement.

- **Inclusivity:** No one is excluded from any part of the child care setting. Instead of excluding a child from an activity because of a lack of persistence, for example, changes are made so the activity can fit the child. Everyone participates fully. Staff use developmentally appropriate practices and a goodness of fit model to adjust areas so all children can feel success.

- **Routines and rituals:** Routines and rituals are used to build a sense of security and stability for all the children. For those who struggle with regularity, routines offer a boost to their biological regulatory systems. Routines and rituals are embedded in daily program practices.

J'amal had been in five child care programs by age four when his grandmother enrolled him at Nature North Child Care Center. He came in the first few days ready for no one to like him, so he used his best "bad" behaviors. Ms. Priscilla did not seem fazed by anything he did. She was kind but firm in a way that made him feel safe. He was used to not getting to play with lots of the toys in other places because he broke things because his hands had so much energy. Instead of saying he was bad or couldn't play, Ms. Priscilla sat by him and helped him breathe five times when he started getting too excited. She had him play next to Chad some of the days, and Chad helped him too, because he showed him where to put the tiles so they wouldn't fall down. After a few weeks, J'amal felt happy to be here. He still needed to breathe or take a break sometimes, but he was learning to slow down a little more. Most important, he was making friends for the first time.

## Goodness of Fit and Behavior

Behaviors in young children that adults view as challenging may simply be a reflection of a child's dominant temperament trait. As we have seen, some children are easygoing and others have a temperament that is seen as more difficult or includes behaviors that can be considered difficult as well. One way to understand temperament and behavior is to consider *goodness of fit*. Goodness of fit refers to how compatible an environment is with a child's temperament. We want the environment and the child's personality to work together so a child will experience positive outcomes in development as well as relationships in child care. When we refer to the environment, we are including the physical setting as well as the people in the setting.

### Temperamental Considerations

At the Center for Inclusive Child Care, coaches who are specifically trained in inclusion practices and are working in child care programs sometimes hear from teachers that the reason for expelling a child is that there is not a "good fit" between the program and the child. While it can be true that a program's environment will not meet a child's needs in some situations, rarely is the child's temperament by itself the determining factor for any behavior. For example, if a child has high distractibility and the child care program is in a large, open area with few or no designated spaces for specific activities, he is going to have difficulty staying focused or engaged because of all the action and open spaces around him. This might be true of a before- or after-school program that uses a gymnasium and cannot change the architecture of the space. Another example would be a child care program whose philosophy is very child directed with few scheduled activities, which can be hard for a child who needs structure and routine with a consistent schedule.

Eileen K. Allen and Glynnis Cowdery (2012), authors of *The Exceptional Child: Inclusion in Early Childhood Education*, put it this way:

> Consider, for example, a child who is active, independent, constantly curious, and into everything. This child may be seen as troublesome, a behavior problem, and a candidate for frequent punishment by . . . [those] . . . who hold high standards for order and routine. On the other hand, energetic, adventuresome . . . [caregivers] . . . might view this active, into-everything child as highly rewarding. They might go out of their way to reinforce, nurture, and respect the child's efforts at exploration and experimentation. (477)

Given this, we see that goodness of fit is not always about space, programming, or even the physical structure of a program.

What impacts goodness of fit more often is conflict between the personalities of a child and the adult in the child care program. The expectation should be higher on the adult to make the relationship work. Children, as we have talked about earlier, come to our programs very inexperienced in behavior, social competencies, and emotional reaction, and they look to the adults in their lives to teach them appropriate behaviors and social skills through positive guidance. For example, a three-year-old with low regularity isn't refusing to eat lunch at noon and complaining of hunger at one thirty because he wants to disrupt a teacher's schedule; he is not biologically regulated yet. He may never be well regulated and eating every four hours, but right now he needs support in slowly getting into a better schedule for eating. It may mean having snacks out for children who aren't hungry when everyone else is. Before you think to yourself that you could never have snacks out all the time, think about the reasons why it isn't feasible and the benefits of doing it. Then consider if there is some other way to make it work. Goodness of fit requires us as the educators to try new ways to meet temperament challenges.

## Adapting Programs to Be a Good Fit

Adaptations to the environment that help a child learn better regulation while also satisfying a biological need like hunger need to be weighed against arguments that it will create a mess or everyone will want to do it. Most of the time, once the novelty wears off, children who don't need snacks won't participate in snacktime.

Most of the time, your space can be adapted to meet diverse temperament needs of children by moving objects like bookshelves around, using sound-muffling materials, keeping space well organized and materials in clear bins, or using visuals supports.

Unless it fundamentally changes or alters the purpose of the child care program, changes can be made daily in how you deliver programming to meet children's learning and behavioral needs. Goodness of fit should include an ongoing assessment completed by teachers to make sure all children are being included regardless of where they land on the temperament sorter.

Jackson was a fussy infant without any real schedule for eating or sleeping. His mom had some long days and nights trying to help him get into some kind of routine. When he went to child care, his family child care provider was responsive to his needs while keeping routines that would help him get used to a regular pattern. He wouldn't always nap when the other children did, but she found ways to soothe him and help him relax. At nine months, he is a little more regular than he was as a newborn.

Goodness of fit does not mean that a child has to change himself to fit into the child care program or to the personality of his teacher. Rather, the program and staff must make the adaptations that ensure the child's needs are being met through both developmentally appropriate practice and ongoing assessment of the child care environment.

When the expectations of the child care program fit the child's temperament and developmental ability, then there is a goodness of fit. The child is set up to succeed. This is a goal early educators want for all children.

When the program's expectations differ from how a child participates, the fit can be poor. The important point to note here is that expectations need to be examined carefully to find out whether staff have realistic expectations of what a child is capable of doing.

If a child is enrolled who needs structure and order based on a need to resist change, and the child care program has twenty transitions during the day, there will be a clash before the child even starts. To provide a goodness of fit, the teacher might decide that children can move to activity centers at will or stay longer in one area, accomplishing the same goals but with less movement for the less adaptable child.

Additionally, when the adult in a program considers a child she teaches or cares for to be likable and agreeable, this would be seen as a good fit. It's easy to imagine the flexible temperament style as the type of child who fits into most programs. He is adaptable, has a good mood, is regulated, and can pay attention for the whole circle time.

We know that a strong caregiver-child relationship supports a positive mental health outcome for the child. It encourages the child to attach to the caregiver, which is the foundation of social-emotional growth. However, a poor fit can happen when the temperaments of child and adult clash. Adults are also high, low, or in the middle on the nine temperament traits. For example, a provider who is easygoing might struggle to manage the big emotions of a child with high intensity. Some teachers do not want to adapt to a child who is low in regulation because they think it will require them to make adaptations for all the children. If a provider has one or two children who are high in activity levels within a class of ten three-year-olds, he may think that there isn't time to keep coming up with new ideas for those two.

Because we expect the adult to make goodness of fit, a gregarious teacher working with a child who is shy would not simply assume that the child is stubborn about making friends; instead, she would give the child words to use to enter into a playgroup in order to build those competencies. Goodness of fit may mean that a child makes adjustments too. The teacher is there to guide a child so that the adjustments are in tune with the child's temperament. A child with low regularity can gradually gain more control over his emotional regulation with the help of specific tools like a visual picture schedule, books on feelings, feelings charts, and take-a-break spaces. A child with high intensity can learn the difference in his outside and inside voices. Patience and understanding on the part of the teacher will help a child contribute to the goodness of fit in the child care program.

Mai is three years old and sometimes uses behaviors like crying instead of feelings words to express "I'm tired" or "I don't want to wait to play with the fire truck." When she gets frustrated from waiting, her teacher is helping her practice counting to five before she acts. It doesn't always work, but a lot of the time Mai is able to wait long enough to relax and then think about doing something else.

# 3

## Activity Level—The Need for Speed

*Some children seem to be born at top speed and never slow down. For those children, life is an adventure not to be missed!*

We all know a child who seems to move constantly, whether fidgeting in a chair or running full speed down the hallway. When we talk about a child's energy level, whether high or low, we are referring to the temperament trait of activity level. It is defined as how active or energetic a child *generally* is, because everyone has ups and downs when it comes to how energetic they feel. When looking at activity as a disposition, a child can be highly active most of the time or she can mostly never want to get off the couch.

For example, have you seen an infant who cuddles up in mama's arms and nestles in regardless of what is going on around her? She is very different from the infant who squirms and wiggles whenever anyone tries to hold her, arching her back against the restraint of being confined. One baby may be on the opposite end of the crib when you go in to pick her up after a nap, having moved all over the place while she was sleeping, while another is in exactly the same position where you laid her. These are all examples of level of energy, even in infancy.

As a toddler, the child with high energy might fuss constantly when in the car seat because she wants to be on the move. Another child the same age might go immediately to sleep when the car motor is turned on. In child care, it is challenging when you have two kinds of nappers: the ones who want to go to sleep and the ones who have trouble staying on their mats!

Jimena was on the go from the moment she could move. Even when crawling, she seemed to get into everything before her mom could put it up or away. When she was enrolled in child care, her mom told the family provider that Jimena was a daredevil even at eighteen months. The provider used all her best supervising for safety practices to ensure that nothing that wasn't supposed to be accessed was ever close to Jimena!

A busy infant will likely be a busy preschooler. Some three-year-olds have a hard time staying in one activity center when the next one looks like so much fun! Walking is so hard to do when a little boy with high energy needs to run or jump. On the opposite end, a child with low energy may want to stay in the reading room all morning because reading meets her activity needs and she does not like to go outside to play where much more action is required. Circle time can be hard for a child with high energy because it is a long time to stay in one spot without being able to move around very much. While infants to preschoolers with a high or low activity level will likely learn to adjust to differences in environments as they grow, their basic temperament trait, as we have already learned, will not fundamentally change with their age.

When most of us think of activity as a temperament trait, our mind usually goes to the child who is highly active and energetic more than the child with low energy. But we can all think of some children who can sit for long periods of time and stay with the same task, like building a structure with manipulatives or doing puzzles. These tasks are good for all children for some of the time, but we do not want any child to only play in one area for too long, because he will lose out on the experiences of peer interactions as well as different kinds of learning. If someone does not want to play an active game like Captain, May I? with peers, the opportunities that come with that interaction time are lost, including regulation skill building and play skills.

For successful learning outcomes to occur, teachers want to intervene with strategies for engagement with a child who has low activity too. You want all children to fully participate to the extent to which they are able in all aspects of your programming. For both high and low activity levels, balance the offering of activities in the schedule to allow for active play as well as quiet activities, both indoors and out. For instance, inside the classroom you might have a small climber for active play as well as hollow blocks and yoga balls that encourage large-muscle play. You can also use dancing with brightly colored scarves and other group movement activities. Quiet areas include art, reading in the book area, or building with manipulatives.

## How Does a Child Express High Activity?

As explained above, a child who has high activity as a temperament trait will be busier than a child who is in the middle of the activity range. She has a higher energy level that is expressed through movement, speech, and action. She runs instead of walks and is always moving her legs or arms. Her activity can cause challenges for a teacher who has a room full of other children to keep involved, but it can also be seen as a positive trait. It promotes enthusiasm for projects the teacher is planning and keeps the general atmosphere more charged.

## Challenging Behaviors

For a variety of reasons, the most challenging behavior for care providers is the constant movement of a child with high energy. For instance, it is hard to read a book in circle time if one or two of your children want to get up after five minutes and wander around the room. It distracts the other children from what you are doing, and the two children who leave are missing out on the learning experience as well.

The behaviors of a child who has a high activity level often seem to push providers' buttons. At some point, the child becomes the challenge instead of the behavior, and the teacher may find herself not liking the child very much or wishing for a break from her. High activity level, when clustered with other traits like high intensity and high impulsivity, is in the feisty temperament style. There is no good or bad as a value in the feisty style, but challenging behavior can often be seen in this cluster of traits.

We can face challenges from children's behaviors whether they are infants or preschoolers. For example, an infant with a high activity level can frustrate caregivers if she squirms all the time, making it hard to change diapers or dress her, or if she will never sit and watch as you care for the other infants. Feeding an infant who doesn't like to be still can test patience as well and take much more time. As a child becomes a preschooler, she may be the one who needs reminders to walk instead of run inside so she doesn't knock over another child. A preschooler with high activity may be the one who derails a simple outing to the park across the street because her excitement gets so high that she won't stay in line or follow the rules of walking together.

Part of the problem for a preschooler who has high activity is a lack of engagement in an activity or task. This can be what prevents her from staying in one area for too long. In addition, biologically her body is telling her that she needs to move. A child on the high activity end of the temperament trait may be in motion constantly.

Miquel dumped out everything when he went into the block center. He would open one bin of building materials and, after a short time, empty the container. He would move on to another type of block and repeat the process until the center was covered in a mix of blocks and other materials. Helping Miquel do the cleanup was very challenging as well.

## Positive Behaviors

Not everything about a child with high energy is negative, though. Many teachers will say that the child with all the action brings energy to the other children and encourages interaction and spontaneity. When your child with high activity runs into your room in the morning and gives everyone a high five and says, "I saw a fire truck this morning!" everyone wants to hear about that fire truck. And he can tell a great story!

High activity levels can also keep creativity high and increase thinking outside of the box. A child with high energy may see things differently and want to build a tower out of something other than the same old blocks. As a child grows, if he has been encouraged in this trait, it can take him far in the world. We want high-energy, creative thinkers solving the problems that face this world.

## Effects on the Child's Relationships with Peers and Adults

Activity level is a temperament trait that can exhaust even the most experienced child care providers. It influences our emotions about ourselves, the child, and even the way we perceive how we are doing our job. For example, if you have more than one child with a lot of energy, it may seem that all you are doing is trying to keep up with them and not feeling like you can focus on the children who are waiting patiently for snack or for you to help them with the glue. For a new teacher, it can be frustrating not to know for sure how to handle all this energy. Additionally, if you are the only adult in the room, your time is truly divided between the needs of the child who won't stay in one place and the children who want to hear the end of the story.

As a teacher, your own sense of competence might be challenged when you feel like you are not being successful with a child who has high activity. You may find yourself using negative language with frequency, such as lots of "no" or "Stop doing that, Isaac," when your usual practice is to use positive affirmations with children. Not only can this wear you down emotionally, but it also can take away from your own energy level as you work to keep up with and ahead of a child who is always on the move and doesn't stay in activity centers for long. If your own temperament trait tends to be low-key and relaxed, it is easy to clash with a child who moves all the time and has trouble finishing an art project or eating his lunch.

This is what it takes to keep a child with a surplus of energy engaged:

- **Planning:** having activities in mind that will keep her interest longer

- **Organization:** being ready with a project or task so there is little wait time

- **Resourcefulness:** adding new ideas at the last minute to a game or project to extend interest

- **Attitude:** keeping a positive frame of mind to carry you through difficult times

We want to feel successful when we work with children, and when we have a child that throws us a curveball, it can be upsetting to how we see our own competence. I offer specific strategies at the end of this section to help you work more effectively with a child who has high energy.

Peers also may have difficulty interacting with a child who has a high activity level. Building relationships or keeping a friendship may be hard for a child who simply doesn't stay in play for long with any one peer. A high activity level can interfere with friendships for a number of reasons. For one thing, if the friend tends to be more persistent at play or has a temperament trait that is low-key, that friend will struggle with someone who can't stay in one place to finish a game with him. Additionally, other children may avoid a peer who is always racing around or tends to knock over block towers and leave some chaos in the activity center. Sometimes peers can be frightened by a highly energetic friend who is unpredictable.

A child who flits from this activity to that center can miss out on some of those important play scenarios where skills are learned from peer interactions. The social competencies that children learn in the early years are shared skills that are part of the back-and-forth of interacting, like sharing, negotiating, and working collaboratively. It's also possible that a child who has high energy has learned that some challenging behaviors are effective in reaching desired goals, like leaving an activity he doesn't like early by jumping up and down on a table. Other children in the program might end up receiving the teacher's ire because they think it would be fun to follow the leader and get up on the table too. The child with high energy gets labeled the troublemaker, and to stay out of trouble, her friends decide to stay clear of her. She loses out not only on positive teacher interactions but also on positive peer interactions.

Once a child earns a reputation with her teachers and her peers as challenging, it can be hard to break that cycle. Even very young children figure out what behaviors give them the most attention and reaction, even when those actions are negative. You want to help a child see that who she is as a busy and active three-year-old is exactly who she was meant to be and give her ways she can use that energy in your classroom.

## Effects on Play Skills and Other Development

Not only does high energy impact a child's relationships with those around him, but it also impacts his ongoing development, particularly in play skills, as mentioned above. It is easy to see how the learning that you carefully design in activities can be missed by a child who is involved for only five minutes. We want to help high-energy children learn to stay engaged in sustained play activities for longer and longer periods of time.

In addition to missing out on the specific learning you have planned in the activity, a child with high activity as a dominant temperament trait will also miss out on important social learning when she doesn't stay with her peers for a period of time. It is in participating in the game or the activity or the dramatic play that children learn how to talk about their feelings, how to count higher, how to identify new animals, and so on. They learn from each other. If a girl walks away before her friend gives her the fire truck, she doesn't learn the "ask, negotiate, ask again, solve the problem" process that is part of early childhood social learning.

Many have said that play is the work of the child. Play lets children use their creativity to imagine, to move, to grow stronger in all ways. Play supports cognitive, physical, and language development as well as social-emotional growth. Play skills develop, too, as children interact together, including the following ways:

- learning how things work together by dumping and filling

- growing thinking skills through pretend play

- problem-solving through building with manipulatives

- learning new words in dramatic play and circle time

A child who does not stay involved in a play activity because her body tells her she needs to move may miss out on something important that all the other children are experiencing. For example, the time spent playing with manipulatives encourages a variety of premath or math readiness skills that help children to move from concrete to abstract thinking, but it doesn't happen when a little girl doesn't spend time stacking and restacking her blocks, sorting the long ones from the short ones.

In dramatic play, a child learns to play out a scene about his new baby sister who just came home from the hospital, pretend feeding her and changing her diaper before putting her to bed. It is in these areas of play, by themselves and with peers, that children learn language, cognition, movement, motor planning, and so many other important early childhood developmental skills. A child who doesn't participate is missing out.

## Strategies to Meet the Needs of a Child Who Has a High Activity Level

If you are working with a child who has high energy levels, your goal will often be to keep her engaged for longer periods of time, whether in an activity, peer interaction, one-on-one contact, or learning center. Here are some strategies:

*Reflect honestly on your program's activities as you have them set up. Ask some hard questions of yourself:*

- Do your activity centers and projects meet the developmental range of the child who seems to be struggling with engagement?

- Are your activities too difficult or not difficult enough? Finding the right balance of just-hard-enough can be tricky, but that is often what a child who has high energy needs. If it is too easy, she will walk away after a minute, and if it is too challenging, you will have the same result. Provide a variety of choices for children so they can find that "just right" place.

- Can you tweak the activity to add challenge that might keep a child engaged longer? Remember that because a child is forty-eight months old doesn't mean she will be at the same range as another four-year-old. If her play is not sustained for long, she may need something that is in a range that is either six months younger or six months older.

*Allow for more large-muscle time, including outside play.*

- Give children opportunities to run and push things outside. Let them have as much physical playtime as possible. Using energy in a constructive way will help children learn to regulate their bodies when they need to bring the energy down at times.

- Allow for activities that use muscles and joints, like marching or pressing hard against the wall to "hold it up" for the teacher. Many children need input into their proprioceptive sensory system to feel organized and regulated. *Proprioception* refers to the feelings of motion and position from stimuli from the large-muscle groups and joints (see chapter 10 for more details). Before a child gets to the point of being overstimulated, ask him to do three big marches to the drinking fountain.

*Incorporate a common cue that the child understands for slowing down.*

- Cues can include a visual support, such as a flash card with a yellow circle that symbolizes "slow down," a word that you and the child have agreed to use, or a simple touch on the shoulder.

- Whatever you have decided the cue is, it is important to practice it with the child so he can experience success with it.

- Expect that it won't always work, and don't be disappointed when he misses the cue or ignores it.

- Be positive when she is successful and slows down. This is going to be a gradual process for her to learn to regulate her body's need to be in motion.

***Practice relaxation techniques so the child can begin to regulate his activity level.***

- Help a child learn how to calm himself. Practice breathing deeply a few times. The whole class can be part of breathing exercises. Ask the class to be still, take a deep breath from their stomachs, and hold it for the count of one . . . two . . . and then breathe out slowly, one . . . two. Try this two or three times.

- Show a child where her heart is beating and how it feels when she is sitting and when she has been busy. Help her see the difference. How can she slow down the beats to her heart?

***Examine your quiet areas, like the art center or reading spaces.***

- Keep in mind that a quiet area should be a calmer location than an area for more active play. Look to declutter the space so it doesn't overstimulate. Keep it organized; use clear plastic bins with easy-to-see labeling for supplies.

- Make sure these areas include the interests of the child with high energy. Does he especially like dinosaurs? Have books or art materials that build on what he wants to read or work on.

- Think about what success looks like for this child. Build on that success. For instance, did he stay in the reading center for five minutes today? Encourage him for reading for five minutes. Ask if he can try to do it for seven minutes the next time. Continue to encourage the small steps—which are big steps for him.

***Find ways to incorporate the child's interests into active learning opportunities.***

- Don't be afraid to explore diverse ways of offering the same learning experience using different methods. For instance, does a child have to do a project sitting at a table? How many minibreaks can she take?

- Build on the child's interests to keep her involved. Does she love to explore? Can activity centers become destinations on a "map" she uses as visual support that could include tasks at each site? Your imagination can match hers!

***Offer encouragements to the child as she stays longer without changing activities.***

- Gradually increase time in activities as you watch the child's cues for engagement. Be realistic. If she stays for five minutes today, can you increase interest to seven minutes this week? Then ten minutes? Consider developmental age and stage as well.

- Use lots of positive words and body language so the child knows that she is being successful.

***Be clear on rules, limits, and boundaries.***

- A child with high energy will be better prepared if he knows when and where he is allowed to run or jump. This also gives you opportunities to build success for him by telling him when he is not breaking a rule that he is walking so quietly inside!

- Make physical boundaries where possible. Use your environment to set up natural barriers to long hallways that invite running.

- All boundaries help build children's internal regulatory systems, which in turn will help them control their impulses more and more. Rules that are consistent help children build regulation as well. Each time you refer to the rules in a positive way, you reinforce the biological regulation.

***Be consistent.***

- Do what you say and follow through. Consistency will help children learn regulation skills and build impulse control.

- Keep routines. Your goal is to help a child who has so much energy inside begin to regulate it. Routines build biological regulation, which helps a child understand her body so she can build impulse-control tools.

## Story of Success

Raphael was three and a half when he first came to Ms. Gabriel's classroom. He was a busy boy who often got up from group time after only a couple of minutes and would wander around, talking out loud and disrupting the other children, some of whom wanted to join him. Ms. Gabriel decided Raphael needed some help staying longer at group time, so she got everyone their own mat to sit on, which helped everyone pay a little better attention. She moved Raphael's mat close to hers, and she placed a basket of fidgets like stress balls and tangles between them. He could take any fidget toy when he wanted and play with it during group time. This extended his attention by a few minutes more. She examined group time in general and decided that everyone benefited from more action and so started wrapping it up sooner with some stretching movements. After three months, Raphael is sitting through most of group time and participating with his peers.

## How Does a Child Express Low Activity?

Low activity means a child isn't as active as her peers typically would be. She may use less energy in play or activity centers. The child is more likely to walk than run and may look to others to come to her rather than use her energy to go find a friend. In this section, we will look at how low activity can impact behavior and provide strategies to ensure a child does not miss out on learning opportunities because she prefers to stay in one place.

### Challenging Behaviors

You need to carefully observe any child who does not want to participate with others, avoids using much physical movement, or seems withdrawn, because these can be red flags for issues in physical development, trauma, or a special health need. Once you have determined that it is indeed how she is wired temperamentally, then you can work with her to make sure she is still participating in a developmentally appropriately manner that fits her disposition. Remember, if Mom or Dad tends to be laid-back and easygoing, then you can easily see where their young child gets it from.

> Gilbert, at two and a half, is what the staff at Rainbow Center like to call "chill." Most of the other toddlers in the toddler room are busy pulling out, dumping out, and then refilling the containers of toys in the manipulatives center. Gilbert can sit in the same spot with a stack of foam blocks near him and play with them for a sustained period while all around him continuous movement is happening.

A child who shows little interest in being part of the games outside or playing with a friend in the block area, though, can also raise some concerns for us. While these behaviors may not be as challenging as those of a child with high activity levels, other behaviors can still present difficulties. For example, she may refuse to move to the next activity because it is more physical or outdoors, or she may use isolating play or choose to play with only one friend, limiting her social development. If she is also highly persistent, she may have difficulty moving when an emergency is presented and everyone needs to act quickly.

Such a child may have gaps in her learning if she is only interested in staying in certain centers or activity areas. She won't discover new interests because she doesn't explore or venture into areas she doesn't think she will like, such as the outdoor area where there is more physical play. She may express a lack of interest in the activities that are planned by saying things like "I don't want to do that" or "I'm bored" that can start to grate on a teacher's goodwill. Peers can get on the same bandwagon and decide they don't want to go on the field trip, either, because they want to stay in the room and play in the dramatic play center instead. All of this takes away from learning opportunities and also can set the stage for an erosion in the teacher-child relationship if the teacher begins to resent the child's negative approach to her careful planning.

The child who sits back quietly and doesn't make a fuss may not be disruptive but will surely miss out on important learning activities and the social interactions that we want for all the children in our programs. As with all the nine temperament traits we will look at in this book, each child is unique regardless of whether he has high or low indicators of a specific trait. We want to honor how he sees the world while at the same time making adaptations that will encourage the adjustments we think improve that goodness of fit.

## Positive Behaviors

Underactivity is not usually the reason parents get called by the director of a child care program about their child's conduct in class. We might actually see underactivity in a child as a bit of a relief from the bustling movement of other children who keep us constantly trying to stay ahead of them. You may have even been tempted to say, "She's my quiet one," to others who are visiting the room. Knowing she likes alone time, you encourage her to spend time in the reading center where she likes to sit by herself when she has free choice. If the teacher is aware of a child who prefers solitude and makes sure she gets a mix of both peer interaction and preferred quiet activities, then the child's natural temperament is being supported.

In fact, a child who is prone to less movement and prefers less noise can have a positive effect on the classroom in several ways. Her presence can act as a calming influence on the room, especially if energy levels are on the rise. She can be a natural companion to other children who have temperament traits that are similar to hers. For instance, a peer who is higher on the slow-to-warm trait will be more at ease with a friend who is also more low-key and less energetic.

She can also influence your classroom in other positive ways. For one thing, she may neutralize a noisy snacktime with a quieter voice and model to other children using a quiet inside voice. The child with a low activity level is much less likely to get embroiled in an argument over who gets the toy next or whose turn it is, generating a more peaceful environment where she is playing. She can bring the energy level to a more manageable degree when the atmosphere has become highly charged. Her calmer demeanor can also help other children better regulate their emotions. All this works in favor of the early childhood teacher to keep the program calmer and less reactive.

## Effects on the Child's Relationships with Peers and Adults

Teachers need to be especially aware of a child who, because he isn't creating disruptions and distractions for them, is not fully participating because he tends to be quiet and low in movement, language, and interactions. While this is sometimes helpful for the overall climate of the classroom, it can also mean that the child is losing out on important relationship-building time with his primary caregivers. A teacher may not recognize that a child with low activity level is not being engaged in learning activities since the child is not expressing any challenging behaviors. While the child may be seen as "easy," he needs his teacher to

- encourage him to interact with her through one-on-one time;

- help him feel a sense of belonging to the child care community by giving him "jobs" that encourage him to move out of his comfort zone;

- build an attached relationship with him to support healthy exploration; and

- encourage creativity by nudging him toward new activities and friends.

A child who is low in activity also needs support in building and maintaining her relationships with her peers. Because children will naturally gravitate toward excitement in the classroom, her peers will want to be around the fun and all the activity that is going on instead of playing with someone who isn't showing very much zeal or enthusiasm. If a child tends to be low in activity, she can miss out on the ongoing social interaction that is necessary for learning social skills, much like her peer who is overly active. In each case, the child is not involved in the activity of learning.

## Effects on Play Skills and Other Development

Children who tend toward low activity level as a dominant temperament trait may be content to stay in one activity area, like the art center, and not participate with other children, as we have already touched on in the section above. How does low activity impact their play skills? This is an important consideration because it takes practice with others for children to learn *how* to play, from the early stages of playing side by side to more sophisticated dramas they make up together. Play competencies are learned as children have experiences together, like sharing and problem-solving.

We want children to have some time to themselves; solitary play has benefits for a child as it teaches him self-confidence and how to use his imagination. But as he grows, it needs to be mixed with play with companions. Play is often trial and error for children as they try out behaviors with one another to see what is socially acceptable. Play is the way through which children learn how to communicate and build friendship competencies. Without time spent in relationships, a child who does not learn social skills will struggle with making and keeping his friendships.

Other development impacted by a child's activity level includes gross- and fine-motor skills as well as cognitive skills. Toddlers who use a variety of play objects, like blocks and balls, to move around and build with will learn colors, shapes, textures, and sizes. They also improve their coordination and fine-motor skills. If a child has low activity level, she needs to be encouraged to participate in active play so she will use her hands to roll and catch the ball. She also needs to be an active participant in play centers like the block area, manipulatives, art center, and areas where building, counting, naming colors, and other conversation takes place. The less active a child is in your activities, the less she is learning from her peers and your curriculum planning.

As a toddler grows into a preschooler, using an activity center's building materials helps her learn premath skills as well as language skills as she communicates through creative play with others. Children talk while they play about what they are doing and what they are imagining. This back-and-forth in both language and play teaches word skills as well as cooperation and problem-solving. The child who is only occasionally part of this action isn't practicing the same skills with the same frequency.

Along the same lines, preschoolers who are active participants in outside play with peers will improve climbing and running skills as well as motor coordination. A child who is more sedentary and who doesn't like to play outside isn't practicing jumping and skipping with his peers. This impacts motor planning, which relies on practice. Motor planning is about doing something, gross or fine motor, then learning from it or remembering it as you build it into a new skill. When a child does something enough times, it becomes learned and he doesn't have to try as hard to do it the next time. Without practice and doing, it is harder to move our large muscles into actions like jumping or small muscles into actions like holding a pencil to write.

Children who play both outside games and table games together also learn rules for participating that are part of ongoing social development. They learn "stop-and-go" actions, which promote regulatory skills and impulse control. Children also stimulate their imaginations as they create new play scenarios, even making up their own rules for games. Early educators design classrooms and curriculum with DAP in mind so that all children will benefit from the planning that is done. A child with low energy may need more encouragement than other children to be involved with peers, so finding the balance of participation and quiet time will ensure that she is developing appropriately.

The activities in which children actively engage encourage development along all domains. While a child may manifest a disposition low in energy, we can adjust the environment in ways that encourage movement so that a child's development outcomes will continue to be positive and on track.

### Strategies to Meet the Needs of a Child Who Has a Low Activity Level

If you are working with a child who has low energy levels and does not get involved with other children's play or doesn't want to move to a new learning activity, here are some strategies to build engagement and more involvement:

***Slowly introduce activities or projects that involve more action and energy from the child.***

- Pay attention to when she may be overstimulated and then draw back or give her time to relax.

- Help her learn her own cues for take-a-break time from sensory stimulation.

- Keep your learning goal in mind. Do the finished projects need to look the same, or are there degrees of completion?

***Build the interests of the child into more active play.***

- If a child likes to play quietly with cars, bring mechanic's clothes and props into dramatic play.

- Scaffold her interests into more play that involves peers. If her interest is in reading, pair her with a friend to take turns storytelling. Can that turn into a play for circle time that they can work on together or with a larger group?

***Examine the play areas the child avoids and the ones she chooses.***

- Check to see if the activities are too challenging or below her developmental level in areas she avoids. Work to include more of what she likes in centers she avoids.

- Look for ways to extend play in all areas of the program. As with the child who has high energy, engagement is your goal.

***Don't push a child to be what he is not.***

- Encourage involvement without making it too daunting. A child who has a low-activity temperament will not likely want to be ringmaster of the circus. He might want to be the ticket taker, though.

- Give words or props to the child to use to enter a playgroup if he is hesitant to join in. Practice the words with him, like "Can I put this car on the track too?"

- Use encouragement to help him stay a bit longer with a peer interaction. Build on successes, even small ones.

## Story of Success

Bethany has been at World Learning Child Care for two months, since she was three. She is a very quiet girl and prefers to be in dramatic play with the dollhouse and doll family. She creates elaborate narratives with the doll family and includes peers who approach her to play, but she rarely seeks out others or changes activity centers by choice. Her teacher, Mr. Patrick, began to think about how he could encourage her to use other learning areas more effectively and practice other skills, like art and even movement. He began planning activities where Bethany could incorporate the doll family into other play. For instance, she could put them in a buggy and push them around the center, going to the "grocery store" and "post office" where other peers were playing. He also provided some new books on families, including different kinds of houses in different countries. Bethany has begun to explore more and create her own ideas for taking her interests into other areas. Just last week, she asked Mr. Patrick if she could build an airport with others for a "vacation" for her family.

# 4

# Distractibility—Paying Too Much Attention or No Attention at All

A garbage truck rolling by or a fire engine with a screeching siren is enough to derail a preschooler with high distractibility and send them over to the window instead of sitting in circle time listening to the story.

What do we mean when we refer to distractibility as a temperament trait? Think about it as how long a child will concentrate on a project or pay attention to a task that he isn't especially interested in. We know that most children can stay in play with something they like for a long time given their developmental age, like a child with his favorite cars and a racetrack. The real test comes when we need a child to finish the gluing project we are making for Mother's Day and he wants to get back to the racetrack. A child who can turn his attention to the card and complete it, then go on to play again somewhere else may have low distractibility or be in the middle on this temperament trait. He knows he needs to finish the card (less preferred activity) before he can do what he really wants to do, which is play cars (preferred activity). A child with low distractibility can often stay on task longer than we would expect even in the face of a desired or preferred activity on the horizon. Conversely, a child who just can't seem to stay focused on the less preferred activity, who wants to hurry through or gets upset because he can't leave to play something he prefers, may be a child who is high on distractibility. This chapter will include strategies for both high and low distractibility in children in child care programs.

Distractibility as an innate trait is also influenced by what is going on around the child. The setting he is in will affect his ability to concentrate and tune in. The child care program can encourage concentration or work against it. Consider these features of the physical environment:

- How many toys are available for play?

- How many doors are open to other rooms or activity areas?

- How many messy shelves are visible?

- How many materials/activities are available at one time?

The early childhood setting also comprises the sensory environment. What a child takes in through his sensory system will have an influence on how well he can or cannot pay attention. This includes things such as these:

- room temperature

- noise levels

- smells from the kitchen

- sensory experiences like water or sand table, dramatic play

- lighting

Finally, the environment includes the emotional climate too:

- children fighting over who will have the fire truck next

- a teacher who yells across the classroom for everyone to be quiet

- a child who refuses to transition and is using a tantrum to make his point

- a general sense of insecurity because there has been turnover in teaching staff

## How Does a Child Express High Distractibility?

Even when all the conditions may seem ideal, a child who has high distractibility as a temperament trait may have trouble screening out environmental stimuli. For a very young child, being hungry or needing to sleep can be enough of a distraction to keep him from concentrating. As we have already noted, children have limited life experience at thirty-six or forty-eight months and have not yet developed all the tools they need for concentrating when interrupted or distracted. Some of the strategies at the end of the chapter will address these challenges.

High distractibility in a young child can cause challenging behaviors in child care programs because the child may not stay tuned in to an activity or pay attention to directions. This can result in challenging behavior and impact the relationship he has with his teachers and his peers. It can also hurt his ongoing sense of self-worth, as we see in the young child with a high activity level if he is labeled as "forgetful" or "my ADHD kid." Compounding this can be a sense of nonefficacy because the child doesn't feel competent if he is not finishing tasks or experiencing mastery by being successful. We want all children in our programs to feel successful and competent as they grow and develop, regardless of their dominant temperament traits. Let's look in this chapter at how high or low distractibility can influence development and what teachers can do to help children reach their full potential.

Elle was excited to go to the four-year-old room when she was finally old enough. She knew there would be more time for book nook and writing stories. One thing that is hard for her is when she is reading a book with a friend and someone else comes into the reading nook. She always wants to know what book the new friend will pick and whether it will be something she has already read or something she hasn't seen yet. Then she forgets what she is doing and has to start all over again.

## Challenging Behaviors

High distractibility can be challenging for a child care provider, whether the child is an infant who doesn't finish drinking a bottle because he looks toward every sound that distracts him or a preschooler who has a hard time finishing a job because her focus is constantly disrupted. For a provider, it is frustrating if you feel that a child isn't learning because she doesn't participate fully. We carefully plan programming to meet specific developmental needs, usually based on child development curriculum, and we know that if a child is only getting part of it, she is missing out on learning.

Challenging behaviors occur in child care programs when our expectations for teaching and learning come into conflict with a child's ability to stay tuned in with us. For example, if a teacher is trying to teach a specific task that requires concentration and following simple directions, a child who keeps looking out the window because a dump truck is hauling some gravel past can be frustrating when he keeps asking what he is supposed to do next.

Sequencing is an important development concept for preschoolers to learn, supporting their understanding of patterns and order, before and after. It becomes harder for a child who has high distractibility to master this concept if we can't keep him engaged in activities that practice sequencing. When we need to practice something important, like the three steps for a fire drill, it is important for everyone's safety that children can pay attention to what we need them to do in an emergency.

A child with high distractibility can tune in to the sounds in another classroom and miss the directions on how to finish a project, like fold down the last wing so his kite will fly. When he doesn't have a kite that works, it's disappointing to him and he may not know why.

In any program, leading a group participating in the same activity is difficult if you need to repeat directions to a child who isn't listening. It is easy to lose patience, and the child may not understand why she is in trouble. Being distracted isn't something she does to bug us; it is an internal wiring that makes it hard to screen out all that is around her.

> Chloe has a hard time sitting for very long in circle time in the morning because it is right before snack and she is usually hungry. She can hear Ms. Chrissy putting out the snacks, so she doesn't always hear Ms. Julie tell them who is supposed to go first or how they are supposed to line up. Also, sometimes there are other children in the hallway going outside, and they laugh a lot while they are lining up. She wants to listen to the story because she likes this book, but she hopes they are having oranges today.

## Positive Behaviors

While it might seem like being unable to focus for long or pay attention could only cause challenges for us, in fact high distractibility can work in positive ways for us too. There are lessons we can learn from watching the behaviors of a child whose attention wavers in our programming. For instance, as teachers, it is possible that the pressure to cover curriculum causes us to race through the material and do too much talking, resulting in some children listening marginally or tuning out. We can sometimes forget that our curriculum is a guide for us, not a taskmaster.

How long has it been since you evaluated the sensory input in your environment? How much do you have hanging from the walls and ceilings? How loud is it at different times of the day? It helps sometimes to have a new set of eyes come in and informally assess your room for things that might cause a child to lose focus. Maybe offer to do this with another teacher so you can examine each other's rooms.

A child with high distractibility keeps us on our toes with constant new ideas and possibilities for doing things. Every project doesn't have to be done the same way. Exploring creative ways to get to a similar end is exciting and stimulates all the children.

A child with high distractibility can also be our bellwether, indicating when there are too many teacher-directed activities. Again, stepping back and looking at how much of our day is being led by us and how much is child directed might give us a better balance. A child who loses interest quickly might stay engaged longer in activities that he is choosing.

Finally, a child who has high distractibility can be easily diverted from negative behaviors as well. If the child has other traits like high intensity and activity level and low regularity, he falls in the feisty temperament style. However, it can be seen as a positive that he can be distracted from an inappropriate behavior. For example, if a distractible child was joining with others in yelling, "I want a snack," you can redirect him by saying, "If you help me move this table over there, then we can get out the crackers."

## Effects on the Child's Relationships with Peers and Adults

A child who has high distractibility may, at times, have difficulties building or sustaining friendships with her peers. Friendship skills, as we saw in chapter 3, are necessary to supporting social-emotional development in young children. All children need peers to help them learn the back-and-forth of play and the social behaviors required to be successful in a social setting like child care. They learn from each other by making mistakes with each other, by watching and by practicing with each other through play. For teachers, it can be frustrating to see a child start and stop and start the same project again when it is time to move to something new.

A child who is frequently distracted may not participate in sustained play with others. She may start an activity and then lose focus because of the noise in the room and want to move on to something else. This influences her friendships because she may interrupt the play of others, intentionally or by accident. If she sees a bunch of geese land outside the window and exclaims, "Look at the birds!" as she runs over to the window, the rest of the table may run with her. While a teacher is used to children being drawn to these kinds of interesting events outside the building, it is the frequency of the interruptions that becomes the problem for both teacher and children.

All children move in free play, but the child with high distractibility may not be asked to join in if others think he leaves too much. He may also interrupt the play of peers by wanting to go somewhere else or start something new. This might mean that a friend could become upset with him because she wants to stay in the kitchen longer doing their restaurant play, and she lost her play partner. Peers may avoid him because he tends to get into trouble with his teachers for not paying attention and doing something he isn't supposed to, and they don't want to be partners to that.

It can be frustrating for teachers and caregivers to manage the behaviors of a child who has difficulty paying attention. Trying to finish a project or keep him engaged in circle time can be challenging. He may also interrupt his teacher enough that she begins to see him as a problem child. Teachers do not want to see children through a negative lens, but sometimes some children just seem to push our buttons. It's hard to be reading a book to a group of three-year-olds when one keeps getting up and down, leaving the circle, or disrupting everyone else.

High distractibility can be unsafe at times too. A child who is watching the birds in a tree and decides to see what is going on next to the fence might not be watching for traffic dangers. This means child care providers need extra diligence to keep the child safe.

## Effects on Play Skills and Other Development

You carefully plan your curriculum so that children get the most benefit developmentally from spending their days with you. When your programming is developmentally appropriate (see chapter 2), you have activities and centers that are designed for a child's age and stage so that learning takes place as a child is ready to learn. If a child is disruptive or has problems staying engaged in play in your program, it interferes with the overall learning you have designed for him. It interrupts other development as well.

Children with high distractibility and low engagement lose out on the benefits of prolonged imaginative play with friends. It is within these relational interactions that children learn how to express feelings to each other as well as how to navigate the social landscape. They also learn how to scaffold their current ideas, like about making or building something, into new ideas and ways of thinking.

A child who has problems filtering out what is going on around her may be a child who wanders in play, especially free play. Depending on the child's age, free play is a time for children to practice physical mastery skills like arm and leg coordination while learning to run, jump, or climb. Within the classroom, it promotes creativity and exploration as a child discovers new interests and begins to put ideas together. Playing for sustained periods of time is essential for a child's physical and cognitive development. Keeping interruptions to a minimum helps a child continue learning through her senses.

As we saw in chapter 3, a child who is not involved in our learning activities because of a dominant temperament trait is missing the important skill development that you have carefully designed for them. Later in this chapter, we will present specific strategies for helping a child who has struggles with focus to stay tuned in longer.

> Hazel was painting in the art center because she wanted to make a picture for her new sister, but she heard someone laughing in the block area, so she had to put everything down to run there and see what was happening. Teacher's rule is you have to clean up your paints, and since she left a mess, she couldn't finish painting today.

## Strategies to Meet the Needs of a Child Who Has High Distractibility

If you are working with a child who is on the high end of distractibility, it is important that you look for ways to minimize distractions and encourage engagement. Some specific strategies include the following:

### *Be aware of your sensory environment.*

- Seek to minimize sounds, smells, and noise as much as possible. These can act as major distractors to a child whose attention is easily diverted.

- Some children benefit from noise-canceling headphones for quiet breaks. This needs to be monitored because you don't want a child to miss out on learning either. It can give enough of a sensory break to help a child stay focused longer at other times of the day.

- Keep clutter to a minimum. Put toys in clear bins with labels that include words and pictures. Cover unused shelving or materials from sight. Less is more when it comes to wall and ceiling hangings. Everything can be a diversion when a child has limited focus.

- Use hands-on materials in activities to keep the child involved in a sensory way.

### *Limit the number of peers in centers when possible.*

- Too many children in an area can be too much of a distraction. Try to keep the number of children lower in centers where a distractible child tends to stay longer to build success.

- For this child, you may want to consider a peer partner when a specific task needs to be completed in a certain time frame. Choose a peer partner who has high persistence skills, which can help your child with high distractibility stay longer in a game or play situation. Choose a game or type of play that interests the child with high distractibility to build success again. Be sure to watch for any potential clashes, however, in case the persistent child is irritated by the more distractible child.

### *Group like centers together.*

- Put quiet centers like art and reading next to each other and noisier areas like the block center and the mini-trampoline next to each other to encourage longer, more focused time in areas that are hindered by distractions.

- Listen for sounds the average child might not hear in your space's quiet areas, such as buzzing in the overhead lights or outside traffic. Where possible, use floor lamps and light diffusers in place of fluorescents. Find ways to muffle sounds from outside by covering windows at busy times of the day.

- Allow for breaks so a child can use large muscles or get different sensory input. Help him extend the length of time between breaks with reinforcers like a preferred activity.

### Provide a take-a-break space that has few or no distractions.

- Make sure the rules are clear for this space, like how long a child can stay, if she can bring books, and whatever else you want that space to include.

- Keep the space clutter-free so a child can use it to regroup her sensory system and refocus her attention. It needs to be calming.

- Never use it punitively but rather make it an option as a child's choice when she feels she needs to take a break.

### Provide fewer choices so decision-making is not so overwhelming.

- Give a child two or three choices at most for activities, centers, or projects.

- Consider using a visual support choice board that shows a child two choices at a time for activities.

- Encourage a child when he makes a choice and follows through. Reinforcing will go a long way in helping a child stay longer in activities.

### Be intentional in how you give directions or instructions.

- Make eye contact so you know the child is tuned in to you and your words.

- Give fewer steps and use one direction at a time.

- Help her be successful by completing one task at a time.

- Put materials out as an activity progresses rather than everything at once.

### Help a child regulate himself by helping him understand what takes away his focus.

- Keeping in mind his developmental age, talk to a child about what triggers his loss of attention. You may be able to put in place some ways to avoid his triggers.

- When a child is tired or hungry, he is going to have a harder time staying focused if he struggles with distractibility. Give him words to tell you when he needs a break or a snack to boost his focus.

### Routines and rituals build regulation in all children.

- Better regulation skills will benefit a child with high distractibility by helping her lengthen the time she takes to consider actions. You want to increase the pause between a thought and the action that follows.

- Routines like going over your daily schedule with a visual support build biological regulation for a child.

- Rituals like hello and goodbye songs, cleanup songs, family celebrations, and so on build predictability for children, which in turn supports the growth of regulation and attention building.

### Provide a longer, uninterrupted block of time for child-directed play so the child can become immersed.

- Practicing uninterrupted play will help him build skills to lengthen his attention span. Consider whether a transition is really necessary when this child is playing well.

- The play needs to be in a preferred activity that the child is very interested in so he will stay longer. Think of ways to extend and expand the play by adding additional props or materials.

- Build on small successes. Five minutes increases to seven minutes increases to ten and so on. Tell him that you could see that he was playing well and having a good time.

### Keep the child close to the teacher during activities like group time.

- Seating the child closer to the teacher will help you keep distractions to a minimum and help you keep her focused on your activity.

- Give the child a job during group time, like helping hold the book, so she is focused on being part of the activity.

## Story of Success

Conner is five and has always been curious about the world around him. He sees butterflies out the window and even talks about how loud the wind is sometimes when he is thinking. His teachers have helped him figure out some ways to pay attention when he has to finish a job, like working in a quiet space without so many things around him to pay attention to. He is getting better at finishing what he starts, but he will always be a curious, exploring boy.

## How Does a Child Express Low Distractibility?

Children demonstrate low distractibility by staying tuned in and engaged in an activity or a story you are telling. All children will react to a loud fire engine roaring by, but a child with low distractibility is less likely than most to notice a bird that flew onto the feeder outside the window while he's painting an art masterpiece. This child is usually more flexible because he finishes jobs he starts and can be counted on to listen and follow directions. As with all temperament traits and their ranges, challenges can occur when the environment is out of tune with the child's needs. We will discuss this in more detail in the following sections.

### Challenging Behaviors

While a child with low distractibility is often easier to plan activities and programming around than those who have trouble staying engaged, there are still challenges. This is a child who may not pay attention to your transition cues when it is time to clean up or the social signals from peers who are telling her that they want a turn now. Many of the challenges with this temperament trait surround the persistence of the behaviors that often accompany it. For instance, a child may be so engrossed in her play that she is resistant to leaving it to move to something new, even when her time is up and someone else is waiting for a turn. She likely doesn't see anyone waiting for her to finish. If it is time for all the children to go to a new activity, like if it is time for outside play and she hasn't heard the teacher say it's time to clean up or seen children head for their coats, she is going to make everyone wait while she catches up.

A child with low distractibility who remains focused on a task and likes to complete work could get upset at peers who make noise cleaning up while she is still working. She isn't going to appreciate the friend who wants to tell her about the squirrel the friend saw out the window just now, because she was getting ready to glue an important piece on her project. Low distractibility with a hyper-focus can get in the way of important social interactions. While usually teachers are pleased with children who start and finish their work, it is also important to be aware of whether the child is engaged with other children, making friendships and social connections.

## Positive Behaviors

Low distractibility as a temperament trait is less of a challenge for child care teachers than high distractibility is. It is easier to work with a child who isn't interrupted by the noise and action surrounding an activity, allowing him to persist longer in his tasks or games. Teachers put a lot of time and effort into planning specific projects for children, and it is gratifying when children participate and complete them. The child with low distractibility tends to have a high degree of concentration and focus and likes to finish what he is doing. He usually doesn't get pulled into something going on around him that might divert from what is at hand; for example, he isn't going to join an argument or get pulled into a fight with the two girls next to him about who gets to use the glue next. If a child has low distractibility, it can mean that he has the ability to hyperfocus on whatever activity he is involved in, including creating an imaginative dramatic play scenario with his friends that keeps them all entertained for half the morning.

It's easy to see why low distractibility puts a child in the more flexible range of temperament types since this child is generally more adaptable and go-with-the-flow. Teachers might feel challenges at times because the child is paying so much attention to what he is doing that he isn't paying attention to what the teacher needs to happen next. This can be remedied by the teacher making sure she has the child's full attention before she gives a direction or starts a transition.

## Effects on the Child's Relationships with Peers and Adults

A child who is not easily bothered by what is going on around him will have more sustained playtime to build relationships with peers. This is healthy and what we plan for when we design our physical environments and our activity centers. We want children to build social skills together by interacting through games, projects, circle time, and outside play. A child who can stay focused with two or three friends can create a new game with its own set of rules and names and can play the game over and over. This sustained interaction builds language skills in preschoolers as they all string words together to explain what they will do next, and it supports cognition as they work to figure out how each move should be made and what materials they need. Children like to play with other friends who stay in play with them.

Teachers and child care providers would probably prefer a child who is not easily distracted to one who is overly distracted. It is easier to avoid challenging behaviors with a child who stays tuned in and follows directions!

When a child stays on task and is persistent in finishing what he started, he needs encouragement for his successes. All success helps build a sense of competency. We might be tempted to intervene less with a child who can stay with a task for a long time, but be mindful of how much time he spends alone without supports. Language and social skills enrichment are still part of preschoolers' developmental needs. Consider how you respond to the child who has a great deal of focus versus the child who may have a short attention span. Teachers may need to be intentional in not comparing children or putting a value on one behavior over another.

## Effects on Play Skills and Other Development

As mentioned above, a child who can sustain his attention in play and other activities in child care will pay attention longer and be more involved in learning activities. She will see many benefits to her growth in all the developmental domains.

Social skills are honed through engagement time with peers. Dramatic play that can expand into other play scenarios increases language skills and advances emotional thinking as children grow. Since play skills are learned behaviors, they get better with practice. Playing together helps all children develop language and cognitive skills. Toddlers learn to expand their communication skills through interactions, and preschoolers increase expressive language skills through problem-solving and negotiating. The longer children stay in a play activity, the more they will increase the back-and-forth of their communication.

Preschoolers spend a great deal of time in pretend play with friends, making up elaborate stories with the dramatic play materials. When a child is able to stay focused, this important playtime promotes imagination and creativity.

Building with different play materials like blocks or manipulatives for extended periods promotes physical and cognitive skills. Children who take the time to build a structure with blocks learn how things fit together, how to gauge size needs, and how to estimate numbers, along with colors and shapes.

> Monica and Malu can play together for long periods of time in the dramatic play area. Their favorite story line is to play hospital, where they take turns being the doctor and the patient. Monica uses a small cup from the kitchen to listen to Malu's heartbeats, and then they both take pretend medicine. Monica puts on pretend gloves and checks Malu's teeth and declares her "good."

## Strategies to Meet the Needs of a Child Who Has Low Distractibility

If a child is not easily distracted and can stay focused on an activity, this is generally not a problem for his learning or development. A concern would arise when the child becomes overly focused on a task to the exclusion of other play and does not transition easily. In this case you could use the following strategies:

*Make sure the child has a variety of sensory experiences from which to draw.*

- Watch for exclusions in sensory areas where the child may not feel as comfortable and which she may avoid in favor of staying tuned in to something she prefers.

- We want children to get a variety of experiences. The sensory table is a good place to get lots of varied tactile input, but also look for opportunities to expand her vestibular (balance) and proprioceptive (large-muscle and joint) sensory experiences.

- Examine your dramatic play area for a wide variety of textures and materials to add sensory experiences to dress-up and make-believe.

*Consider giving a child choices for less-preferred activities to be followed by preferred activities to ensure some movement and change in learning experiences.*

- Offer encouragement when he tries something new. Let him know that you are there to help him if he has any questions or problems. Help him feel secure in a different situation.

- Consider allowing more time for a preferred activity when he does try new things. This works best for an older preschooler.

*Ensure that choices for new activities or play include the child's interests to draw him to a different activity center or play situations.*

- If a child rarely wants to leave the reading area, try building a favorite story or book into dramatic play by having him create a play for himself and others.

- Ask the child for ideas. How could you change some centers to be more interesting to him?

*Examine your transitions.*

- How necessary are each of your transitions? Can any be eliminated? Because this child tends to want to remain in an activity until it is finished, you can avoid a challenging behavior by letting him have time to complete what he's doing.

- Make some transitions optional. When children are actively engaged, let them remain in a center to complete a play cycle. Give those who are ready to move the opportunity to go to something new.

***Observe and record playtime for patterns of solitary versus group activity.***

- If you have a child who tends to stay at a task to the exclusion of other activities, be aware of how long and how often he plays alone.

- If you find he is spending too much time isolated from his peers, consider ways to bring others into the activity he is most engaged in. Enlist more social peers to join him with props to extend play.

## Story of Success

Mitchell is four years old and loves to build with Lego blocks. His mom told his teacher, Mr. Charlie, that Mitchell spends hours at home building elaborate castles and towns. It is his favorite area at child care, but sometimes he is so busy building that he doesn't hear Mr. Charlie tell everyone to pick up toys in five minutes. Sometimes Mitchell doesn't even notice everyone else is lining up for lunch! So his teacher is helping him with a special notice that Mr. Charlie calls a "cue." The cue is a deep touch on his shoulder that tells him it is time to start cleaning up. They practiced it a few times so Mitchell would know what it meant. It makes it easier for Mitchell to clean up now and not miss out on getting into the lunch line on time!

# 5

## Persistence—Patient or Stubborn

We want children to stay engaged in a task or play activity for some period of time, either to learn a skill or to develop friendships. When a child won't leave a play area because she needs to finish building the house with blocks, it can mean challenges for the teacher trying to get everyone to lunch on time!

What is persistence? Persistence as a temperament trait refers to the length of time a child might stay with an activity or task before giving up, especially if what they are doing becomes more challenging to them. It differs from distractibility in that it isn't about paying attention but rather about sticking to a task when it gets hard. Here are some examples to consider if you are thinking about a child who may be high or low in persistence:

- How long will a child play a game even when it gets difficult for him?

- Does a child tend to want to finish something she starts regardless of how long it takes?

- Can a child wait to get snack after peers, or does he need to be the first one?

- If she is asked to stop an activity, does she get upset, or does she easily move on to something else?

Persistence can be part of the feisty temperament type, especially when it is coupled with high distractibility or low adaptability. Both high and low persistence can be seen as challenging to a child care teacher because of the behaviors that can be part of the disposition. Persistence can play out in child care in a number of ways. Sometimes a higher degree of persistence is viewed positively if a child stays with a task even when it becomes hard for her. She might be called "patient" and "tolerant." We like to see children stick to a job that is challenging for them and work their way through it to a solution. At the same time, a child might persist in a play scene, like building a fire station with her blocks, where she does not want to leave it regardless of what is coming next in your schedule. She might be seen as stubborn instead of patient.

In the same way, a child with low persistence might be seen by teachers as a go-with-the-flow kind of child who easily moves from one play activity to the next when someone else needs her truck or doll; she might be characterized as easy to get along with. If, on the other hand, the less persistent child becomes easily frustrated and gives up quickly while doing a puzzle, she may be seen as difficult or challenging.

Remember that children get their wiring from genetics as well as the environment around them. So we as early educators can support a child's natural tendency to persist or not persist by the way we set up the child care classroom and activities. Specific strategies for classroom management follow at the end of each section.

## How Does a Child Express High Persistence?

Adrian is a two-and-a-half-year-old who loves having books read to her and "reading" them herself. She has favorite books that she wants to read first, but she likes new books too. She can snuggle for a long time on her teacher's lap, listening to the stories and talking about what she sees on the pages.

Persistence can be a wonderful thing! We see the benefits of persistence in people we work with who can be counted on to finish a job, even when it becomes hard or tedious. It is a trait that helps relationships through tough times or great difficulties. We can see positive outcomes for children who naturally persist.

Temperament traits like persistence impact decisions we all make as we grow, but children have fewer options for making choices using their innate character. That is why the early educator plays such an important role in viewing temperament through a positive lens for the sake of the child's view of self. We want to give all children the chance to grow into their best selves. When we think about children who have high persistence as a dominant trait, we often use positive adjectives like *stick-to-itiveness* and *patience*. A child with this trait will stay with a project regardless of interruptions by his friends or feelings of frustration when he can't quite solve a problem.

Persistence is about sticking with something when it gets uncomfortable or hard. We want children to be able to learn skills to stay with some things that are important for them to finish, but we also realize that some children will become bored or lose interest more quickly than others. As teachers strive for goodness of fit, adaptations can be made to help the child who can patiently wait and stay at something past the need to transition and also help the child who gives up a bit too soon.

## Positive Behaviors

Teachers see many positive behaviors when a child has high persistence as part of his personality. The child may be seen as very patient! This is a child who can stay with a task that you have given him and finish it, even when there are distractions or it becomes harder than he first thought it would be.

When a child continues with an activity for an extended period of time, her learning is extended as well. If she is sorting blocks, for example, she is building her fine-motor skills in picking up the blocks and stacking them, as well as her cognitive development in sequencing, problem-solving, mathematics, and creativity. A child is more apt to discover different ways of doing things when she persists at it. For example, she might start painting with her fingers and discover that if she mixes some colors together, she makes new colors. All this exploration and discovery is important to a child's ongoing cognitive development.

A child with high persistence is likely going to stay in play longer with peers and engage in more creative play with them as the drama they create together expands. She may be an encouragement to other children to stay and complete a project as they watch her keep at it and finish it. She is probably going to succeed in reaching goals, either those she sets for herself or those that have been set for her, depending on her developmental age and stage. This becomes a lifelong skill. A child with high persistence has a good attention span. She will play on her own for long periods of time without needing help or asking for assistance. All of this makes for a child who is usually easy to care for, especially if she has other temperament traits in the flexible temperament style.

## Challenging Behaviors

High persistence in a child is often seen as part of the flexible temperament type, but it can also be seen as feisty depending on how rigid the child's persistence is. For example, as seen in the above paragraphs, a child who sticks with a project despite having to start over or having difficulties can be seen as a child with high flexibility. However, a child who persists to the point of resisting help or change can seem intractable to a teacher. The high persistence could result in refusal to transition or do what the teacher requests, escalating the behavior to a power struggle. In this case, a child might be seen as having some challenging behaviors, for instance, such as continuing to persist at an activity when it is time to transition to a new activity. This could lead to behaviors like refusal to change or meltdowns at the prospect of change. A child may have difficulty moving on from play to the next part of the schedule if engaged in a preferred play activity.

Persistence could be inflexible for a child who is comfortable with one area, for example, the book nook, and who wants to read the same books over and over again without moving to a new center like art. This inhibits other learning from taking place. Cleanup can be a difficult time if a child does not want to end play. As a result, power struggles can ensue between the teacher and the child over putting away the puzzle he wants to do one more time.

High persistence can be a challenge to teaching staff when a child cannot seem to regulate it or control it. For example, persisting at a project is often a preferred behavior from a child when we want to finish a get-well card for the director, but when a child wants to keep tweaking it and making it better, that can frustrate both the teacher and the child. Children with high persistence need to know when something is "good enough" so they can move on to a new project. When a child demonstrates an unwillingness to change, it puts tension between the child and the staff who need to keep their schedule and keep all the other children engaged. Strategies in this chapter around high persistence include helping a child regulate his innate need to persist with skills to help him transition and change. Remember, again, that it is a positive when a child likes to stay with a job until she finishes it, which we all love to see in our classrooms and child care programs!

> Kaim, who is almost four, fell to the floor and flailed his arms to demonstrate his unwillingness to leave the art center. He was still painting at the easel board and wasn't ready to go outside yet. His teacher turned to her assistant with an exasperated look.

## Effects on the Child's Relationships with Peers and Adults

A child with high persistence may have mixed relationships with her peers, depending, again, on how much impact her ability to change has on her behaviors. Peers may appreciate a friend who sticks it out in an activity and finishes a job. If two children are working on a challenging puzzle, it helps when they both are motivated to finish it. Working together makes the play more fun. They also learn by helping each other find the pieces they need to fit into the puzzle. A child who doesn't get frustrated easily is more comfortable to be around. She is more predictable and not prone to outbursts that are unsettling to a peer playmate.

On the other hand, a child who doesn't want to give up on a project when her friend wants to go to another play area or when a friend is waiting for her turn could foster disharmony because of her persistence. A child with high persistence who refuses to change can cause disruptions for the whole classroom if everyone is waiting on him to go outside or to the snack table. If this happens often, other children may become angry at him for always making them wait.

A child with high persistence can come into conflict with the schedule of a child care program if he stubbornly sticks to an activity or project until he is ready for change. For a few reasons, a child resisting transitions or change can cause difficulties for child care providers. Transitions are a common part of the child care day and the daily schedule. Some programs move children more than ten times a day. Disruptions can set the whole day off course. They can delay activities or cause some things to be missed altogether if a teacher is spending too much time in struggle with a child who won't leave the block area. If the child care provider begins to see the child as "stubborn," she may begin to think that the child is just pushing her buttons by refusing to cooperate. This sets the stage for relationships to deteriorate.

A teacher may find a child who has high persistence as a positive influence in her child care program too. A child who likes to complete work has a decidedly encouraging influence on the whole classroom. A child who persists in finishing a difficult puzzle, for example, may be a friend that others like to play near because she is a good helper in completing hard jobs. A child with high persistence will often be more flexible in playing in a variety of areas, content to try different things. She may be less likely to rush into situations that are dangerous or outside the rules, which can be a good influence on all the children in a program. This child will likely wait longer for snack or to go outside, helping a busy teacher with lots of children to get ready to go out or prepare food for.

> Stephanie and Malik are playing restaurant in the dramatic play area. After five minutes, Malik decides to be a firefighter with his friend Carl. Stephanie, however, elaborates on her restaurant with pies and cakes, persuading two other friends to join her efforts. Malik returns as a cashier, and all four children play out their drama for the rest of free-play time.

## Effects on Play Skills and Other Development

All nine temperament traits can impact a child's ability to play successfully and develop in ways that are optimal to overall growth. Anytime a child looks like she is "stuck" in a play pattern, as might happen for a child with high persistence, there is a concern that the child might not be interacting in ways that promote social competence and other skill sets. For example, if a child prefers to play alone with manipulatives, it may be hard for a peer to come alongside and join her. She may reject a friend who doesn't follow her lead or play in the same pattern. If a child is persistent in staying in one task for a long time by herself, she may resist the teacher bringing her into a play circle with others. By not joining in, she is not learning what the teacher has planned for the group that day. The child can lose some important social-skill development when she is not interacting with others typical for her age because she is not exchanging conversation, learning how to express herself, or practicing understanding the needs of someone else. On the other hand, if a child sticks with a task even when it becomes challenging, she learns self-efficacy. This is an important emotional milestone to be mastered. She feels competent in her own skill and is likely to share her knowledge with her friends because she feels good about what she can do. Helping others, too, promotes her sense of accomplishment and self-worth.

> Ayan likes to work on puzzles and can play with them again and again. Her teacher knows Ayan loves puzzles, so she brings in a more challenging puzzle every few weeks so Ayan doesn't get bored with the same ones. In this way, her teacher encourages her to try something new that is still something Ayan enjoys. Ayan is delighted to have something new to problem solve, even when it takes her longer to finish a new, harder puzzle.

## Strategies to Meet the Needs of a Child Who Has High Persistence

As you work with a child who has high persistence, your goals will be to help him adapt more easily to change and develop some tools for transitioning more smoothly. Here are some strategies to try. Consistency in any strategy is important, but keep in mind that something might work for a while and then a different strategy may be more effective.

### *Avoid power struggles by being aware of the triggers for a child who may have difficulty with transitions.*

- Observe the child, looking for patterns or times of day when transitions may be most difficult. Sometimes hunger or sleepiness can make transitions more difficult for a child who resists changes. Consider letting some transitions go and allowing the child to stay with his activity to finish it.

- Offer a snack if a child seems resistant in the morning or close to lunch. He may be more apt to try something new if he is biologically regulated.

### *Incorporate visual supports.*

- A visual picture schedule that you go over each day will help a child know when movement is expected.

- Refer to the picture schedule whenever a transition is coming up so the child has enough warning time to get ready for the change.

- If a child struggles more with a particular transition, create an additional visual support like a small cue card to show her she must get ready for it. The cue card can incorporate any visual as long as it is clear to the child that it means "time to clean up," or whatever you have both decided.

### Support a child's emotional literacy.

- Make sure a preschooler has words he can use to replace aggression or other challenging behaviors when he is frustrated.

- Practice with a child what he might say when he gets upset because a peer interrupts his play. Give him words and phrases.

- Help a child understand his own emotions about wanting to persist. Phrases like "I know that you feel upset when you have to finish something you want to keep doing. What can you do to feel better?" can become a problem-solving exercise for older children.

### Extend her interests into other areas so she will want to try something new yet familiar.

- If a child only wants to play in the block area, take building materials outside and see what can be created in that setting. Or allow a car to move to the sensory table for an underwater raceway.

- Pair the child with a friend with similar interests and give them a project to do together in a different activity center than she usually goes to. For instance, if they like airplanes and like to stay in the manipulatives area, have them do an art project where they build an airplane out of art materials.

### Whenever possible, make sure enough time is allowed for a project or activity to be finished before it is time to transition to something new.

- When it is important for a child to stay until something is finished, this planning on the teacher's part can avoid a standoff when the next move is supposed to happen.

- If a child feels he was successful in completing his activity, he is going to be more apt to move on to the next activity.

- Encourage his success! Especially when he finishes or when he tries something new. Praise goes a long way in building a sense of confidence to try new things.

### *Avoid labeling a child as stubborn or obstinate.*

- A child will internalize the tone we use when we use words like *stubborn* or *obstinate* to describe her. Encourage her with positive words about her ability to stick with something.

- We never want to make a child feel less than other children or that there is something wrong about who she is as a human being. Avoid comparing her to a child who moves more easily than the highly persistent child.

- Labeling can rub off on the other children, who can start teasing or bullying from what they hear the teachers say.

### *Build on the positives of high persistence.*

- Being persistent may seem challenging at times, but it is a positive trait in many ways because the child is engaged in projects and wants to do a good job.

- Persistence means a child completes work, doesn't get discouraged easily, and sets goals that he finishes. This is a child we want to have as a leader in our classrooms!

- Because he likes the challenges, a child with high persistence doesn't usually get frustrated with tasks. This can be a good example to the whole room! As children grow older, this is also a positive trait for many experiences, such as finishing homework or practicing piano.

## Story of Success

Jackie is two and a half years old and has been in the same family child care program since she was an infant. Her child care provider, Ms. Marisol, knows that Jackie can be easy to care for at times because she will sit and "read" her books without being bothered by what is going on around her, even when the two infants are crying because it is time for their feeding. However, at other times, Ms. Marisol knows it is hard for Jackie to put down the books even when they are transitioning to snack or outside play. So Ms. Marisol has been practicing with Jackie in small ways to help her find a way to finish reading time. One strategy is to give Jackie three books, and when Jackie is finished, she comes to Ms. Marisol to see if a change is occurring, and if not, then she can read three more. So far, Jackie seems to be a bit more tuned in to what is going on in the child care setting around her.

# How Does a Child Express Low Persistence?

Low persistence means that in the face of an obstacle, a child will give up easily. The obstacle might not even seem challenging to a peer or caregiver, but if the child perceives it as hard, he will move on to something else or perhaps engage in challenging behavior. This can be seen in a child who cries when a puzzle is too hard and throws the pieces down, stomping away. This trait also relates to how a child reacts to being bothered while completing a task. Some children with low persistence will not be able to handle an interruption, such as someone who wants him to come see what they just built with the building bricks. He may instead become agitated at his friend and give up because he isn't able to handle those kinds of typical interruptions.

## Challenging Behaviors

When a child is low on the temperament scale for persistence, it may be hard for her to manage her emotions when she becomes frustrated because something is hard for her or she doesn't know how to do it. Frustration can cause a child to act out with aggression or show withdrawing behaviors to get away from the work. A child may dump all the blocks out and, when it is time to clean up, become overwhelmed with putting them all away again. This can result in tantrum-like behaviors or a power struggle with teachers when she doesn't want to put it all away.

A teacher can begin to resent a child whom she may perceive as unwilling to try or, worse, noncompliant. It is hard to turn back an attitude that is negative about a child, even when we know that is how a child is naturally wired.

## Positive Behaviors

On the positive side, a child with low persistence who moves from activity to activity may have high creativity and energy that spreads across the classroom. It is always fun to have a child who wants to try something new or do it in a new way. It can help us see our programming through fresh eyes. A child with low persistence may develop stronger social competencies because she relies on friends to help her and she knows she can count on others when she becomes frustrated.

Low persistence can be seen as a negative or a positive, depending on how it manifests in a child's behavior and the reaction of the adults to the behaviors. We can encourage a child who doesn't always stick it out to learn more patience through the strategies that will be presented at the end of this section. We can also help him with coping skills when he becomes irritated at a peer who keeps interrupting his work.

At two and a half, Gilbert hasn't mastered some of his developmental milestones yet because he doesn't stay with one set of toys or activities long enough to develop skillfulness. His peers spend time sorting and stacking and naming some colors. Gilbert can stack two or three blocks before he moves on to the cars or baby dolls.

## Effects on the Child's Relationships with Adults and Peers

Because many temperament traits, when they are dominant, can present challenges in relationships, we have to carefully consider why we as teachers are feeling a certain way about a child and be aware of our perceptions of a particular temperament trait. Low persistence can trigger a provider's feelings that a child is uninterested or hard to handle, which then can lead to a spiral of negative interchanges.

Teachers can become frustrated while trying to keep a child engaged who doesn't stay in a play center or activity. It is difficult to carefully plan a project and then have a child only marginally participate. The child who wanders can also be frustrating to providers. This can disrupt other children from their play and cause chaos in a classroom if everyone starts to follow her lead.

If teachers are not aware of temperament, they might begin to think the child is pushing their buttons on purpose and become unable to return to a positive place with the child. On the other hand, the teacher may find this child helpful in getting everyone on board for a change in plans or a new idea. Having someone who embraces change can encourage everyone to try something new.

It can be hard to build strong peer relationships between a child who has low persistence and other children who might want to stay in play longer. A child who gives up too soon can stop some of the fun. This is also a child who needs your help in learning how to extend his ability to stay with a game or in an activity with others through increased regulation and practice.

A child with low persistence who becomes easily frustrated could use behaviors like hitting or throwing toys at peers when he can't finish something. Children will tend to avoid another child whose behaviors are unpredictable. A child who sees that others won't play with him may become even more frustrated and repeat the challenging behaviors unless an adult intervenes with new behaviors.

A child with low persistence may ask for help over and over from peers before attempting to finish by herself. Depending on the age of the children, this could become a barrier to friendship if she is seen as not trying or interrupting all the time. On the other hand, it gives children a chance to help others too. Many times children like to help one another finish a project or get the last piece of the puzzle for a friend.

## Effects on Play Skills and Other Development

Early educators know that play is an important part of how children learn and develop. If a child doesn't learn tools for longer engagement in play, she misses out on important developmental mastery that comes through playing and connecting with her peer group. It is very difficult for a child to learn the rules of a game if she leaves just as it is getting started. Staying in the activity teaches important skills that are lost if the child becomes frustrated and wanders away. If a child spends too little time in long, extended, creative, and explorative play, she will miss important skills like learning to inquire, explore, negotiate, and wonder.

Play promotes cognitive skills too. For example, play with blocks provides children with opportunities to learn a number of scientific and mathematical principles. If a child is not staying long in the block area, he may not be using counting skills and naming colors with peers. In addition, the block area encourages other kinds of development, like imagination and fantasy play as children build airports and hospitals and then act out dramas there. A child with low persistence moves from area to area, never fully engaging in that play and gaining the accompanying developmental benefits.

We expect different levels of persistence in toddlers than in preschoolers, based on age and experience. Low persistence is a temperament trait, but we don't want to forget that temperament traits are influenced by the environment too. We want all children to begin to learn skills that help them meet challenges effectively, whether in play or in learning, while still honoring the essential dispositions that make them uniquely who they are.

## Strategies to Meet the Needs of a Child Who Has Low Persistence

Low persistence can be more of a struggle for child care providers than high persistence is. Low persistence will have more impact on how smoothly a program is running, especially if you can't avoid disrupting behaviors. Low persistence and high distractibility often go together. A child may be easily distracted, and then because of low persistence, she will give up easily or become frustrated because she was interrupted. If you are working with a child who gives up easily when encountering a challenge or difficulty, here are some ways to build their endurance:

***Look for sensory stimulation or environmental triggers that might interfere with a child finishing a task.***

- Reducing clutter can help a child stay focused longer. Look around your room for any unnecessary equipment or materials laying out or in piles. Can they be organized more neatly or, better, put away out of sight?

- Are noisy areas next to quiet spaces? Keep the reading nook next to a quiet center and the noisy block area by the trampoline. If you want a child to stay engaged in a project longer, reduce the noise in that activity area where possible.

- Reduce the number of posters and pictures on the walls and mobiles hanging from the ceiling. We tend to keep hanging these throughout the year without realizing how much sensory information this is for a child to take in when she may already have a hard time filtering out sensory input.

- Consider using muted colors on your walls and other areas wherever possible. Bright primary colors activate the brain and arouse children. Soft colors relax and calm, helping a child stay tuned in.

### Consider the physical arrangement of your play areas.

- Put toys in clear plastic crates with easy-to-read labeling using both pictures and letters. This makes cleanup much easier and less overwhelming because it is easy to see where everything goes.

- If there are multiple options for games in a play room, a child may discard one game when it becomes too hard and pull out a different one, until the floor is covered in cards and tiles. Limit the number of games that are accessible at any given time to one or two.

- Be organized, especially with projects you want children to do. Have everything ready to go when children come to the table. Avoid wait times that encourage a child who lacks persistence to move on to something else.

### Be aware of a child's biological needs as triggers.

- Be sure the child isn't thirsty or hungry when trying to complete a project or finish a game. Provide a snack if the child needs one to stay tuned in, or keep a healthy snack bowl out at all times.

- Crunchy snacks like pretzels help a child focus better. Sensory input to the jaw helps increase attention and focus. Keep crunchy snacks on hand for a child who seems to be nearing the end of her attention cycle.

- A tired child will be less able to stay focused. Check with parents about sleep patterns. A nap or a short visit to the take-a-break space might help improve persistence.

### *Offer fewer choices so the child is not overwhelmed by too many options.*

- Examine your activity centers with a critical eye. What could you clean out? Do you have too many toys, making it hard for a child to settle on one?

- Consider utilizing a choice board with a child who has low persistence. A choice board is a visual tool that lets a child choose between two or more pictures of food, activities, and games. It helps him make decisions more easily, which also helps him feel more successful.

- Rotate his preferred toys with less preferred ones so he tries new things. Realize the less-preferred item or activity may be short-lived, so work on small increases in time spent doing something new or different.

### *Break tasks into smaller parts so the child can reach success sooner.*

- Give encouragement when a child achieves each task.

- If the task is something the child does frequently, think about making a visual of all the steps for her to look at and use.

### *Work in sensory breaks for a child when he is doing a longer task.*

- Give a child fidget toys from a fidget basket. Allow him to hold them throughout circle time or while doing a project. Fidget toys can extend attention and focus. Offer variety in your fidget basket to meet different sensory needs.

- Engage a child's senses with diverse experiences. Let the child who struggles with staying engaged have longer time at the sensory table or in dramatic play. This may help organize his sensory system in a way that helps him focus longer and stay tuned in because his body is not telling him to keep moving on.

### *Build activities around a child's interests.*

- A child will tend to stay engaged longer in an activity that she is interested in. Observe where she stays longest and try to incorporate some of that interest into other areas. For instance, if she likes dramatic play and uses the doctor dress-up props, bring books about vets into the reading room or circle time.

- Small successes build into greater successes. When a child doesn't give up, that is an achievement for her. Encourage her when she sticks it out. Use positive and specific language about her finishing a job. Ask how it makes her feel.

***Remember that this child is naturally wired toward low persistence.***

- He can build tools to regulate his impulse to quit with adult assistance and support, but he will likely be a less persistent child. Keep in mind that he is not willing to stick to something that isn't interesting to him.

- His disposition also makes him more open to trying new things and seeing things in a different way. See this in a positive light. How can you build on his creativity and spontaneity as a positive influence on your program?

## Story of Success

Camila is almost four and has a hard time sitting through story time. She usually likes the stories, but she also wants to see what is going on at the sensory table. If she sits next to her teacher on her carpet square and she gets to pick her favorite foam ball to hold, she usually pays attention to the whole story. Her teacher is always so happy when she sits and listens the whole time!

# 6

## Adaptability—Resisting or Embracing Change

Change is inevitable in early childhood programs, whether it is new children or new teachers. Even minor changes can happen on any given day, like a friend who has to go home sick. Some children go with the flow and nothing shakes them. For others, even a small change can ruin the whole day.

Adaptability as a temperament trait is displayed in a child's level of reaction to changes and transitions over time. Does he react with great distress when it is time to move to a new center activity, or does he quickly pick up and move on to the next event with no fuss? Even as adults, we may find we are happier when we have a schedule and plans because that suits our style. Others of us may find that we like spur-of-the-moment happenings—or at least we don't get upset with last-minute changes. Adaptability differs from approach/withdrawal in that adaptability is more about the duration of the reaction, whereas approach/withdrawal is about the intensity of the initial reaction. Children may be low, high, or right in the middle on ease of adaptability. High or midrange adaptability would typically put a child in the flexible temperament style, especially if other traits like positive mood and high approach are part of her personality. A child who is low on adaptability, in combination with high intensity and low persistence, would be in the feisty style. As you think about a child's adaptability, here are some indicators to help you see where a child might land on this temperament trait:

- Does a child quit easily when you give the signal for cleanup time? Or does she dig in and say no?

- Do changes in the daily schedule cause crying, or does she like to do something out of the ordinary?

- Does she adapt quickly to a different approach, or does it take a long time to get used to something new, like moving the sensory table outside?

Children experience change in many ways every day in their child care settings too. Factors that make up changes in the early childhood setting can include the following:

- newly enrolled children

- new and substitute teachers

- changes in the schedule like field trips or skipping outside play

- new foods, different sounds, and other changing sensory experiences in the setting

- unpredictability in schedules and routines

- moving to a new age-group classroom

For all children, consistency in child care, including staffing and programming, is an important indicator of quality. Consistency has a major influence on attached relationships and feelings of security, which impact how effectively a child learns. The ease with which a child can adjust to changes or not is at the heart of adaptability as a disposition. In child care, adaptability is important to recognize as a dominant trait because it can be the reason for some challenging behaviors. Behaviors a teacher might see related to a child's natural ability or inability to shift to something new include the following:

- easily transitioning to an unexpected change with little warning

- clinging to the provider when something new is introduced

- resisting a move with a tantrum or other refusal behaviors

- accepting a new food or item without any fuss

- crying when asked to move to a new activity

High and low adaptability can both bring positive experiences to peers and providers, depending on the ability of the environment to be responsive to individual needs. Challenges can occur as well when the environment is not set up in a way that gives children with low adaptability more structure and those with high adaptability experiences to create and explore.

Sam's mom told his family child care provider that he was an easy baby she could take anywhere and he never fussed. As an eighteen-month-old, he plays with almost any toy around him, and if someone wants what he has, he will quickly move on to something else.

# How Does a Child Express High Adaptability?

As we look at the nine temperament traits, we see that each one has strengths and challenges. Child care providers often see challenges in a child's ability to adapt because an early education program has many transitions during the day that require a child to accommodate change. Remember that adaptability is part of how a child is wired genetically, but the environment can have an influence on how well a child learns adaptive skills. As early educators, we can help children extend their ability to manage change through the way we set up our programs.

On the other side of this disposition is a child with high adaptability, someone who can roll with whatever might come up and adjust to a change quickly. He may also be a child who is high on approach and seen as easygoing or flexible. He probably eagerly meets new friends at preschool and asks them to play with him right away. High adaptability is a trait that is usually seen as a positive in early childhood settings.

## Challenging Behaviors

Challenging behaviors are less likely with a child who easily adapts and embraces change. Early educators might like a room full of these flexible children! There are a few things to keep in mind if a child is highly adaptable, though.

A child who is quick to accept change may also be one who doesn't stop and think through what the change might mean. We want to make sure we are teaching all children impulse-control skills so they can make good choices. He may rush into situations that can pose dangers if he is not watching. Active supervision is as important for him as for all the children in a program, even though you might not think of him as a child who runs or is overly active.

Children who are less adaptable may ignore or avoid a child who adapts more easily. She may be so easy to get along with that older peers could take advantage of her good nature, tending not to share or resolve conflict in a fair way. Being aware of the social interactions of all children will help alleviate any child being left out or taken advantage of by peers and gives the teacher the opportunity to build social competencies for all.

## Positive Behaviors

As mentioned above, high adaptability is usually seen as a positive trait because adjustments to changes and transitions are done very easily. It doesn't take very much time or energy for this child to feel okay in a new situation. High adaptability is grouped in the flexible temperament style, especially if a child is also high on approach and positive in mood. In child care, it is easy to see how this could manifest in behaviors that benefit the whole classroom.

Generally a child with high adaptability is one who takes change in stride and isn't easily ruffled. For instance, if there is a substitute teacher in the classroom, it doesn't affect his day or demeanor. He may take the lead in moving children to a new activity or area because he is eager to try something new. As an infant, this child may fuss less when a change in schedule happens and he has a bit more wait time than normal. He doesn't need to be the first one fed or diapered. As a preschooler, he may be the first to try the new vegetable or start the new game because it's an adventure to him. Others often follow.

> Asha and Miguel are best friends in Ms. Imani's three-year-old room. They both like to do lots of the same things, like go up and down the climber. If someone else wants to join them, they like to show the newcomer how to do it or let her go ahead. If the climber gets too busy, they just start chasing each other around the playground. Other children like to play with both of them because they are easy to get along with and like to share.

## Effects on the Child's Relationships with Peers and Adults

A toddler or preschooler who has high adaptability will likely have good relationships with peers because he is flexible and easy to get along with. Everyone can picture the child that plays well with friends and hardly ever gets into a disagreement over a toy or what someone wants to do next. This is often the child who likes to try new things, so moving on from the dollhouse over to the fire station because someone else wants it is an opportunity instead of a problem. Additionally, he is a child whom others enjoy being around because he doesn't tend to use aggressive behaviors to get his way or to object to changes in what he is doing.

However, a child with high adaptability may be more apt to be affected by peer pressure because of a child's tendency not to hesitate before taking action. This is something for teachers to be aware of with older children if cliques have been forming in the program. This child may "go along" just because she is easygoing when it may be harmful to her social development or the overall classroom climate you are building. Additionally, a child who is easygoing may need to learn some skills to assert herself so that if she does want to do something, she has the words to express herself so she isn't always giving in to others. Usually though, children with high adaptability are easygoing and tend to be fun to play with because of their flexible nature.

A group that includes children who have high adaptability makes a classroom run more smoothly, especially when unexpected changes to routine occur. The atmosphere in the child care program can derail quickly if one or more children refuse to transition or engage in tantrum-like behaviors because they do not want to change.

Teachers enjoy children who go with the flow and transition easily. Instead of needing to think through avoiding a power struggle with a hard transition, the teacher knows that the change will be made without difficulty. Because the adaptable child can shift from activity to activity easily, it gives the child care provider more time to help a child who struggles with low adaptability or high distractibility. Teachers will also find that if a child is expressing a challenging behavior, he will be easier to move to a more appropriate behavior because of the child's ability to change more quickly than a child who is less adaptable.

> Tiara was sad when she learned that the guinea pig, Chester, wasn't in the classroom anymore. Teacher said it had to go home with the bus driver. However, at circle time, everyone got to talk about what they thought the new pet should be, and Tiara told Teacher she wanted a rabbit or another guinea pig. Even though she missed Chester, she was so happy that no matter what it was, she would have another pet friend when she came to preschool.

## Effects on Play Skills and Other Development

As stated earlier, a child with high adaptability is a child whom other children want to play with! It's easy to be friends with someone who has the following characteristics:

- changes easily

- is willing to negotiate

- doesn't mind switching toys

- moves easily from center to center

- doesn't use aggression to get his way

Both play skills and social competence are easier to develop for a child when he is a preferred playmate. If a child is flexible and easygoing, he will naturally have more play interactions with others. The more opportunities a toddler or preschooler has to engage in activities with others, the more opportunities they have to develop.

Toddlers with high adaptability learn a variety of new skills because they will explore more than one favorite area. This will enhance motor skills as well as growth in language and communication skills.

Preschoolers who adapt easily will tend to experience more friendships, learning new social behaviors through playing with a wide variety of children. They typically do not play with only one play partner but with the whole room.

Toddlers and preschoolers who move around with ease may be less challenging for caregivers, but if they give in too easily to peers who want to take their toys or crayons, they may not learn to stand up for themselves. Be aware of bullying that might take place because a child is so flexible he loses his place too often or gives toys away so often he rarely finishes with them.

Strategies at the end of this section will help you focus on the strengths of a child who overall is a positive influence on peers and your program. Making sure her needs are met may take more intentionality because she is not demanding in the same way other feisty temperament types call attention to demands with challenging behaviors.

## Strategies to Meet the Needs of a Child Who Has High Adaptability

If you are working with a child who is highly adaptable, he may be a flexible and easy part of your classroom. You probably don't need to make a lot of adaptations to your programming or environment, but as you consider his needs, your strategies should be around ensuring his safety, minimizing risks, and making sure he is included by others:

*A child with high adaptability may go into new situations more impulsively than a peer who would hold back a bit.*

- This might mean the child rushes forward at times without thinking. He needs skills in pausing before taking action. One example is for him to practice counting to three before doing something he isn't sure about.

- He may benefit, too, from practicing waiting for short periods with you to support more self-regulation. For instance, count to five before giving him his snack. Let him count with you. "One, two, three, four, five. Here you go! That was a great wait!" Be aware of his frustration levels as he learns to wait.

- Be aware that even a flexible, easy child still needs active supervision. Because he tends to adapt well to any given situation, you may forget that he can also be impulsive and still needs a watchful eye.

*Ensure that peer interactions do not disadvantage the child who is more willing to change or give in.*

- A child who is highly adaptable sees less problem in changing a toy or giving up her spot. A child that is less adaptable might use this characteristic in her friend to stay in her area and not share when her turn is up. We want all children to learn to share and have time to play regardless of their natures. Intentional observation on the teacher's part will ensure that there is consistency and fairness among children.

- Watch for signs that your highly adaptable child is not staying in any one area for any length of time. It might be that her adaptability is working against her being able to finish out play or a game she started. She may be following a less adaptable friend around because she's so easygoing.

***Make sure the highly adaptable child is not the one who always has to change.***

- If you are asking for children to go to a new center or play area, be aware that the adaptable child may be trying to please because he is so flexible. While it is tempting to use the flexible child as your initiator for new projects or games, also give him a chance to have sustained play in one area as well.

- Teach children how to recognize and name their feelings. A child who may be ambivalent about leaving can be helped by being able to say, "No, I want to stay here." Encourage him when he asserts himself in a positive way.

***Build on the interests of the highly adaptable child as well as others so she is able to stay in an area and extend/expand play situations.***

- Ask her what she likes to do. Build those interests into an activity center or project. Even when this child is not a concern for not finishing or losing attention, it honors her temperament when you embed her interests into play areas.

- Make sure your interest areas matter to all the children. Children will stay longer and remain engaged in more sustained play if it is something they are interested in.

***Don't assume that because a child is flexible, he doesn't need you.***

- A child who is highly adaptable has figured out how to make things work. The adults need to know when he truly is ready for a break or needs support to advocate for himself with peers. He may not ask you, so make sure you are observing him on a regular basis to make sure he isn't being bullied or giving up a turn with reluctance. You may simply need to ask him, "Did you want to leave dramatic play already?" and give him a chance to answer, even using some prompts like "It looked like Alice asked for her turn and you weren't ready to be done yet."

- He may inadvertently be the child that always has to wait because you know he's so easygoing. Strive for equity whether a child is feisty or flexible.

Be aware of the child who isn't expressing challenging behaviors and isn't taking attention away from everyone else.

## Story of Success

When four-year-old Jasper enrolled in Ms. Lili's preschool program, he was easy to get along with and rarely made a fuss about moving to a new center or sharing a favorite toy like the fire truck. After a couple of months, though, Ms. Lili started to see that Jasper would hesitate when asked to give up the computer before his time was up, but he would still comply with a peer. She talked to him about this one day after she saw it occur and asked him how he was feeling. He said he didn't feel good when he had to leave before his turn was over, but he didn't want someone to be mad at him. He and Ms. Lili worked on some phrases to help him tell a friend that he wanted to finish his turn but his friend could watch until his time came. Jasper felt good about this. Ms. Lili saw him use the strategy the next day, and when his friend said, "That's okay, I'll come back later," Jasper gave Ms. Lili a big smile.

# How Does a Child Express Low Adaptability?

Low adaptability combined with other temperament traits like low approach/withdrawal and negative mood fit into the temperament cluster we referred to earlier as fearful or slow to warm. Temperament types are not good or bad; they simply indicate a child's tendencies toward particular behaviors. The fearful classification refers to a child who is more reluctant to change when a new situation is presented and also tends to react with less energy in transition situations. Low adaptability has more challenges than high adaptability in child care programs because this is a child who resists change. In early childhood settings, there are usually frequent changes in everyday programming, from transitions to new toys to new projects. A child who has a dominant temperament trait of low adaptability will need support from her provider to manage fearfulness and worry over what she doesn't know is coming or changes that she can see happening.

## Challenging Behaviors

Challenges in behavior can occur when a child's dominant temperament trait is low in adaptability and he has difficulty with unexpected changes in the schedule or even just routine movement within the child care schedule. A child with low adaptability may also be low on approach/withdrawal and simply likes to wait and see before starting anything new or approaching a new person or activity. Likely this child would be in the temperament type referred to in chapter 1 as fearful, meaning he needs more time to warm up to new people or situations. The combination of some traits makes for more difficult behaviors at times, especially if the setting has not adjusted to his needs to improve the goodness of fit.

This temperament trait will bring more challenges to the child care teacher than a counterpart with high adaptability does. Keeping in mind that the child comes to us naturally less open and welcoming of change can diffuse our feelings when we are becoming frustrated by some of these more difficult behaviors.

Tantrums or meltdowns can occur when a child refuses to leave an activity center or make a transition. New teachers or new students may be slowly and cautiously regarded by a child with low adaptability. She may react by displaying anxiousness or aggression to the change in people. Withdrawing behaviors are not uncommon for a child who feels uncomfortable and wants to remain where he is.

> Connor has great difficulty when he has to leave any play that he has started when it is time to move to another part of the child care day. His usual response, at three years old, is simply to throw himself down and cry, saying, "No, I won't!"

## Positive Behaviors

As teachers, we can view the interactions of this child in positive ways as we help him feel more secure and less anxious. Low adaptability means children need more structure and routine. We may become more aware of our program's need for improved structure through the eyes of the child who resists change. Implementing more consistency in programming benefits all children in developing their regulatory skills. This is a preventative strategy for challenging behaviors.

Low adaptability for a child can also mean that child isn't going to rush into something that might be dangerous or off-limits. Caution can be a good thing! This is something we can celebrate about this young child.

## Effects on the Child's Relationships with Peers and Adults

A friend's low adaptability can be difficult for peers to understand or accept unless there is guidance from the adults. Adults need to help the peers of any child who struggles with social interactions or uses behaviors that interfere with play to feel safe and secure. While not calling attention to a specific child, setting up the emotional environment so everyone feels safe is part of developmentally appropriate practice (chapter 2).

This involves, as much as possible, not disrupting the schedule for all children because one child is having trouble moving. Stay as consistent as possible, using routines that are the same each day. Use positive teacher talk like "This is a safe place" and "I'm going to be here tomorrow" to set a tone of security and well-being for children.

A child with low adaptability needs peer relationships but may find that her anxious feelings about change get in the way of interactions with someone she really likes to play with. As mentioned earlier, her friends may also tend to shy away from her and put a pause in building a reciprocal friendship.

If a child with low adaptability uses behaviors like crying or withdrawing because she doesn't want to go outside or eat something she's never had before, this can cause upset or anxiousness in the children trying to play with her. Most children move easily from building a block tower to changing it into a racetrack. A peer who tantrums because she doesn't want the tower to be knocked down may encourage challenging reactions from other children, like knocking it down anyway or throwing a block at her. The next time these children play together, their first tendency may be to react negatively because the pattern has been set.

Friendship competencies are an ongoing work of early educators, especially in the preschool years. Intentional emphasis on kindness, patience, and helping a friend who needs us can be circle time topics for older preschoolers. Support to both the child with low adaptability and peers in play-skill development will help everyone have more positive relationships.

Low adaptability can be hard for teachers who are trying to manage a classroom of children who move with regularity from center to center or from activities like lunch to quiet time. If a child is very reluctant to transition from an area he is particularly comfortable in, he may get stuck in a pattern of challenging behaviors to avoid the change. Remind teachers that challenging behaviors continue because they work for a child. Giving a child new skills so that he feels more comfortable with change will be one of the strategies presented at the end of this section. We want children to feel successful and staff to feel confident as well.

## Effects on Play Skills and Other Development

The previous section dealt with many of the challenges that might present themselves for peers who play with a friend who isn't able to adapt to change well. Children at different ages and stages will sometimes be active in playing together and will also go in and out of play with peers. If a peer is consistently unable to be a positive play partner, his ability to learn from play will be compromised.

The exchange of ideas and language takes place in the reciprocity of a play scenario, like playing doctor and patient or mom and dad. This exchange is limited when one child refuses to change his position, for instance, if he always has to be the doctor. At some point, his friend may decide she isn't going to play with him anymore because he doesn't take turns.

Different types of play are important for different types of development. For instance, mastery play is when children repeat an action or play at an activity until they have learned the skill. A child who does not adapt to change may stay with a task long after she has mastered the skill without moving on to greater challenges. This could slow ongoing development.

Sensorimotor development is dependent upon experiencing new input to taste, sound, touch, smell, and sight. It engages a child's senses and encourages her movement, balance, and other motor skills. A child who refuses to try something new is missing key sensorimotor development opportunities. We want children to move through play stages, from playing alone to eventually playing in cooperation with others as they organize more sophisticated play activities. A child who struggles with changes in routine, new people, and new settings is a child who will want to stay more fixed and not challenge himself in new types of play.

> Jasmine at age four is very particular about what she will wear to child care because she doesn't like anything that has a texture that is heavy or coarse. Her mom says she has had a preference in dress since she started picking out her own clothes. When she fell outside on the playground and tore her pants, her provider tried to put a spare pair of pants on her. Jasmine would have none of it. She screamed about how it felt until her provider put the torn pants back on her.

## Strategies to Meet the Needs of a Child Who Has Low Adaptability

A child with low adaptability will show more challenging behaviors because, by nature, he is less equipped to handle changes and transitions. Fortunately, in early childhood the provider has the ability to adapt the environment in many ways to avoid or lessen the impact of low adaptability on behaviors:

***If the child prefers to stay in one play area, encourage movement to another by letting him take a favorite item or toy from one area to the next.***

- It might mean changing rules you have about toys staying in their centers, but consider how much you and the child both gain if it eases the transition.

- A child who only wants to play with the cars can move a car to the block area, or even to art to draw a picture of it. Get creative with building on his interest. Ask the child how he could use cars in another area of the program or incorporate cars into a project you want him to work on.

- Remember that the goal is to extend this child's ability to make a transition or change. Keep the long game in mind. What will help him move more successfully without using a challenging behavior?

*Try to increase the child's frustration tolerance, based on developmentally appropriate practice considering her age and stage.*

- Give the child words to express herself when she is frustrated or feeling other emotions. Have her practice talking through situations where she becomes upset or anxious, like having to leave a game when she isn't ready.

- Once she learns to recognize when she is getting upset, help her learn new ways to pause the reaction. This could be taking five deep breaths or counting from one to ten. Whatever the strategy, she needs to know it and be able to use it. She only needs one or two tools for dealing with her frustration.

- This takes practice and will not work overnight. It is a skill she must learn through doing. Offer encouragement for any effort she gives.

*Resist putting this child in situations out of his comfort zone.*

- Forcing a child into social situations doesn't help him become more outgoing or approachable. It will likely result in a challenging behavior like crying or withdrawing.

- Have realistic expectations for a child who is low on adaptability. Don't expect this child to be the first one to welcome a new friend to school. However, he should still be expected to be pleasant and kind to peers. He may need help in learning these social skills.

- Create a buddy bucket or a co-project between the child who is resistant to change and a new child using an area that is of high interest to the child with low adaptability. For instance, if he is very interested in insects, put together a buddy bucket with a book on insects, plan a project to make a drawing of bugs, or have them work on a small ant farm together.

- Encourage the child for all efforts made, no matter how small the progress. The goal is to help him try new things or transition with less anxiety.

*Reduce the number of transitions in a day whenever possible.*

- Examine your schedule with a critical eye and consider how many moves you ask children to make each day. How many are necessary? Can you reduce some?

- Limit the wait time within the transition by giving children more to do while the wait is taking place. If you have a child who has problems with transitions, bring something that is a favorite of hers to wait with.

- Think about what the teacher's role is in the transition and what your expectations of the children are in each transition to avoid frustration on either side. Do they need to be quiet? Do they have to be in a line? How flexible are you with how the transition happens?

- Teach children how to transition. What are your expectations for behaviors during a transition? Let the children know how they should do it successfully and let them know they did a good job. Encouragement goes a long way in getting children to repeat positive behaviors.

### Make transitions fun!

- Engage children, especially those with low adaptability, as much as possible with songs, marching, finger puppets, and sensory toys like fidget toys.

- Monitor transitions for signs that they are overwhelming a child who has problems with changes. Be proactive about a child who might hit another out of frustration by putting him in front of the line. Prevent a meltdown by intervening using the tips in the previous bullet point.

- Give transition cues to a child so he knows ahead of time when one is happening. Use a song or a visual cue card like a yellow circle.

- Make sure a child has time to finish an activity before he has to move on to avoid challenging behaviors caused by his frustration that he has not succeeded or finished. If a child lingers for a long time over a task, figure out ways to cut out some steps and still complete the job.

### Use timers for a child who has low adaptability for moves and changes.

- A visual timer helps a child who has difficulty leaving an activity to know exactly how much time she has left to complete her play or task.

- A timer can also help a child stay in a task that is less preferred or new to her if she knows it is only for a certain amount of time. Gradually work a child into a change if she is very resistant.

### Use and practice a visual picture schedule.

- Make sure children always know what is coming next by referring to your picture schedule throughout the day.

- Avoid surprise changes as much as possible. If a sudden event comes up, try to prepare the child who doesn't adapt quickly by talking about it with him so he feels safe.

- Go over any planned changes in the schedule, like a field trip, a few days ahead of time with the child. Put it on the picture schedule so everyone sees it and is aware of it for several days.

***For a child with low adaptability, an individual picture schedule that she carries with her can be helpful.***

- Make a smaller version of the day's schedule that can be looped onto a child's belt or carried in a pocket.

- This will help a child know and prepare for what is coming next during the day. It will help her feel secure and react with less surprise to transitions.

***Give a cue for change for the child who has difficulty changing.***

- If the problem is changing to a new activity, create a visual or auditory cue for the child. It could be a hand on his shoulder or a small red square that you hold up.

- The key to success is practicing it with him so he understands what it means. Since the understanding of time will vary with a child's age, be consistent on when you use the cue each time so he begins to regulate according to the cue.

***Understand that this child is wired to have low adaptability.***

- Temperament is part of how the child sees and reacts to the world around her. If we continue to use natural temperament as our lens, it will lessen our frustration with a child who resists us at times.

- We can increase a child's ability to tolerate changes by slowly introducing her to new changes as long as she feels safe and secure. Consistency in routines helps a child try something new because she knows she can count on other things staying the same.

## Story of Success

Sharice came to Bright Stars Preschool when she was two and a half and has been there for a year. She doesn't like to try new things, including new food at snacktime. Her teacher lets her keep a transitional object—in Sharice's case, a stuffed bunny—in her cubby space. She can go talk to Bunny and hold it anytime she wants, but it has to stay in the cubby. Sometimes when Sharice is doing something she is worried about, she goes over to Bunny for a hug. Knowing that Bunny is always there comforts her.

# 7

# Approach/Withdrawal—Quick to Join or Wait and See

One child can come into a new child care setting and know all the other children the first morning! Another child might sit back and observe the first week before taking the big step of entering the dramatic play area with others.

The temperament trait of approach/withdrawal refers to a child's initial response to new people or new situations. It is similar to adaptability because both refer to a child's reactions to changes or transitions, though approach/withdrawal is more about the initial reaction to something new, whereas adaptability refers more to how long it takes to adjust to a change. Ask yourself these questions about a child's tendency to approach or hold back:

- Does she hesitate to meet a new teacher or new friends in the classroom? Or does she eagerly go up to new people and say, "Hi, do you want to play with me?"

- Does she need time to settle in before she starts to play, or does she come right into the room and start racing her cars around with a buddy?

- Is saying goodbye to her parent in the morning tearful and hard, or does she give a quick wave and head off to the playground?

If a child is closer to the approach side of the trait, he is going to be eager to meet a new friend and embrace an outing he hasn't tried before. If she is closer to the withdrawal side of the temperament trait, she is going to hold back to make sure of a situation before joining in. We also use the terms *low approach* and *slow to warm* or *slow to warm up* for withdrawal. These words refer to that tendency not to rush in, but to wait and see, to hesitate before going to someone or something new.

For early educators, approach/withdrawal has many of the same challenges and positives as adaptability in a young child. A child who is high on approach will see a new child care program as an adventure! Toddlers and preschoolers will be looking for opportunities to make new friends. High approach is part of the flexible temperament style. Withdrawal as a dominant temperament trait means a child will be less impulsive and will want to watch from the sidelines before deciding on a course of action. Withdrawal is a trait that is in the feisty cluster of temperament style.

When we consider approach/withdrawal in infants to preschoolers, we may notice that a child who is closer to withdrawal will likely also be a child who is low on adaptability. When we refer to this trait as *slow to warm up*, we mean that he isn't going to go with open arms to a stranger. For instance, as an infant he may prefer only a few well-known people to hold him and comfort him. As an older toddler, he may not want to go to new people or even people he knows who aren't in his very close circle. This can create turmoil if a child care teacher changes in the infant or toddler room. A preschooler may tend to hold back before engaging with new peers or the puppets in the puppet show. He likes to wait and see what might happen next.

On the other hand, if a child is high on approach, she may go into new situations or meet new people with enthusiasm. She may be the one who runs to the new child and gives him a big hug on his first day in child care. She won't be shy about being the firefighter's helper in group time or telling the new teacher that she likes her shoes. She will go up to a visitor and tell them her name or that she's in Ms. Becky's class.

Our early childhood environments can meet the goodness of fit needs for a child's approach/withdrawal disposition with intentional practices. A child who is high on approach will have less to actively adapt to because he will naturally be sociable and flexible. A child who is closer to withdrawal will need an environment that supports a sense of security through consistent routines and schedules.

A child who is high on approach has many positive characteristics that teachers will appreciate. This child is creative, energetic, and friendly. Transitions don't bother her, and neither do some of the hiccups that might happen in a typical child care day. She is going to be the flexible temperament type because she is likely also highly adaptable and has a positive mood. The challenges for providers come more from a child who is low on approach and slow to warm.

> This is Michael's first day at First Start, Best Start Child Care. Michael is three. After Mom drops him off and finishes with her goodbye, he runs straight over to where a group of children are climbing in the playground and says, "Want to play with me?"

# How Does a Child Express High Approach?

For early childhood providers, having a child who is on the high end of approach makes the climate of the program feel friendlier and more inclusive because the child goes out of her way to make everyone feel welcome. Approach is about being open to a new experience, so when a new child is enrolled, as in the previous example, a child who is high in approach will be full of curiosity about the new classmate. Additionally, she will be positive about changes you may bring to the program right from the start, so her enthusiasm will help bring other children on board as well.

## Challenging Behaviors

Finding challenging behaviors in a child who has high approach and is flexible is rare. However, a provider needs to be aware that a child who is quick to approach can also put herself at risk because of her impulsivity. She is less apt to consider danger in a situation or in a new person. She may approach with openness and not be fearful of the unknown. She needs guidance in how to make safe and healthy choices.

Acting with impulsivity can result in challenging behaviors if a child isn't also learning regulatory skills. For instance, running to hug a new friend might be overwhelming to that child, especially if the new child tends toward withdrawal. It's easy to knock over someone who isn't ready for a bear hug.

Because she likes to explore new things, safety may be a concern if she rushes into a dangerous situation. For instance, running ahead of the group could put her in traffic danger.

A child with high approach could be so busy socializing that he doesn't get down to business when a task needs to be completed. Because of his flexibility, a reminder to finish the get-well card will probably be all the prompting he will need.

All children across the nine temperament traits will display a challenging behavior from time to time because they are learning what social expectations are and how to get their needs met. Sometimes these two things are at odds with each other until a child develops strong social-emotional skills to navigate the social scene and also express her feelings.

## Positive Behaviors

A teacher will see several positive behaviors in a child who is high in approach.

The child who is quick to approach is often very outgoing and sociable. She is probably friends with everyone. She is probably also high on adaptability, adjusting to new teachers or children easily, as well as to changes in the schedule or activities. Generally, she meets change head-on with enthusiasm.

A child with this temperament trait tends also to be a hands-on learner who dives right into a new project or task. She will tend to be an explorer and will not need to wait for others to see what is coming next. This child sets a positive tone for the child care program because she is happy with whatever is going on around her.

A child who has high approach may also share a disposition of positive mood as well as high adaptability. It is easy to see how he fits into the flexible temperament type because he adapts so easily to what is going on in the environment. A child who is high in approach is likely going to be eager to try new things, to experience a challenge, and to meet new people. Typically, this child is easy to have in the early childhood setting.

> Emily is eighteen months old and loves her toddler classroom. When she enters in the morning, she waves bye-bye to Daddy and then makes her way across the room to see Jason or Clara in the kitchen center.

### Effects on the Child's Relationships with Peers and Adults

Children with high approach will have few problems in their relationships with other children in the program or with their teachers. They will have a positive influence on a child care program because of their tendency to meet challenges with openness, moving full speed ahead.

A child with high approach will make friends with peers easily. He will get to know the new kids or the new teacher because he is an investigator and explorer. He will be the child who approaches a new student and asks what his name is and tells the new student his name and what his favorite game is.

She will also encourage other children to try something new by being the first one to do it! She adds a lot of energy to a child care program, especially when something new and exciting is about to happen. However, since she may go full throttle into a new situation without hesitation or fear of danger, peers may be frightened by her lack of fear or follow her without question. Being aware of each child's unique disposition will help you know whether a child with high approach is more measured in responses or tends to be more reckless. If this is the case, intentional and active supervision will help you keep everyone safe.

The relationship between the child who is flexible and her child care provider is going to be fairly smooth because of the general cheerfulness and lack of fuss on the part of this child. While this book is intended to help providers struggling with challenging behaviors, it is important to remember that temperament is not something a child chooses but something that is innate. A child who is high in approach is naturally going to be easier because of her personality, but she still needs guidance to learn what behaviors help her to be successful in the social world of child care.

## Effects on Play Skills and Other Development

Play is an adventure for the child with high approach. Unlike a child who doesn't want to change activity centers or try a new toy, this child will go full throttle into something new and different. Likely she hasn't seen a game that she didn't want to try, even if she changes the rules halfway through because they seem like more fun.

Her play skills will be influenced by this positive temperament trait in several ways. Because she likes to meet new people, she will practice play skills in new ways with different peers. High approach is not always about being social, however; she is also able to play alone without being frustrated or feeling left out. Solitary play gives her time to examine a play problem at length and come to a solution on her own, gaining a sense of self-efficacy from the success. If a game or toy has changed from how it was in the past, she will want to explore or investigate. Play helps her learn problem-solving and encourages her imagination, among other skills. Because the child with high approach is often willing to do new things, learning and development are enhanced. She isn't always repeating the same movements or playing with the same materials.

A child with high approach enjoys new sensory experiences like foods, textures, sounds, and smells. Sensorimotor development increases the more a child uses her senses to interact in the world. She is making discoveries about how the world relates to her body through actions that incorporate her senses. She will likely have a broader expressive and receptive language development because she interacts with everyone she comes in contact with. Since she does not typically hold back in relation to new people or new projects, she benefits from the experiences that you as the teacher are planning, including community members visiting the classroom or family members of children participating in day-to-day classroom activities.

Cognitive skills are enhanced by experiences. The child who is high in approach is seeking experiences and adventures. We see this in a toddler who goes up to an adult and shows him her stuffed puppy or a preschooler who can't wait to talk to the special guest at circle time. These children are always seeking and open to what is coming next.

> Abigail is five years old and has been in her child care center since she was an infant. She will be transitioning during afternoons to a prekindergarten program, which she will attend full-time next year. She will be going with six others in the center. She told her

teacher that she can't wait to go on the bus to the new school! She has so many questions about the bus ride, what will happen when she gets to the new school, and who her teacher will be in that classroom. She said to Ms. Rachel, her current teacher, "Don't worry, you are still my best friend."

## Strategies to Meet the Needs of a Child Who Has High Approach

For the child who is quick to approach and eager to investigate new situations and meet new people, you will want to set up an environment that supports his inquisitive nature while keeping him safe as well. Here are some strategies:

***Make sure you check in with the child regularly to ensure that learning as well as social-emotional goals are being met.***

- Observing and recording growth in developmental domains should be done regularly with all children in a program. It may be easy to forget a child who doesn't express her needs because she is so easygoing, but just because she is friendly doesn't mean she may not have developmental gaps or needs.

- She generally isn't going to make a fuss for your attention, so you will need to be intentional in "tuning in" to her with one-on-one time to ensure that she is mastering milestones.

- A child who is very friendly may be overlooked for developmental issues because her social side is so prominent. Observe and record so you know whether her social skills are on track for her age and stage as well as other developmental domains. Her ability to adapt can mask a deficit in a developmental area.

***Give a child who is high in approach opportunities for sensory experiences to promote continued learning.***

- A child high in approach will tend to be an enthusiastic, hands-on learner. This will allow for diverse sensory experiences, including a wide array of materials in dramatic play and in the art center. Create projects that promote your learning goals using a variety of materials that he can use to create and explore.

- Offer a wide range of activities that stimulate touch, smell, sound, muscle sense, and balance. A child high in approach is very social and may need encouragement to remain in a play situation to gain skills.

- Encourage sensorimotor development through his social side that wants to engage and play with friends. Make sure your dramatic play area has lots of different textures to draw from. Work off his social ability to teach through partner play and group activities.

### Give her opportunities to use her friendships skills.

- A child who is highly approachable is very sociable and outgoing. Even though she makes friends easily, she still is learning social skills, so help her use words when needed to join others. Help her not to rush into someone's play but to approach peers and gain permission to join them. Books on friendship skills can be helpful.

- Give her opportunities to invent new games and, when old enough, write plays for the classroom. This builds on her strengths and encourages other development, such as language and imagination.

- Consider having her be your greeter in the morning to use some of her social energy. Think of other areas where her social strengths can be used to build a positive climate in your program. Encourage her natural abilities to be outgoing and friendly.

- Partner her with a new child to help him meet everyone and feel welcomed to the child care community. This will also strengthen her sense of competence and self-esteem.

### Always be aware of potential hazards for the child who is not afraid of risks.

- A child with high approach will be an explorer, eager to go into new situations. Being aware of his nature will help you design more effective ways to keep him safe.

- Active supervision will be critical for a toddler who has little fear of new situations. You might tend to keep an eye on the child with high activity or high intensity rather than a child who is flexible and easygoing, but he also needs to know there are boundaries and limits he must stay within.

- Help a preschooler learn ways to pause before acting to improve regularity skills. Practice pausing strategies like "Stop and breathe three times," "Count to ten," and "Stop and look for Teacher."

### Be sure she knows your rules about safety.

- Friendliness and openness to new people is a wonderful attribute, but it also means the child isn't afraid of strangers. Go over your rules regularly with all children but especially emphasize them with a child who tends to approach any person.

- Post your rules where everyone can see them. Use pictures with the words. Rules as a visual support help children learn regulatory skills that are important for impulse control.

### *Help a social child develop skills for persisting and finishing tasks.*

- Because he loves new things, he may move quickly from activity to activity. Build his interests into activities and play areas to keep him engaged longer. Encourage him when he stays at a play area or project.

- Focus on his strengths. Since he is a social butterfly, he may want to be a teacher's helper throughout an entire activity or project. This will keep him in the activity to the end and also ensure he is learning.

### *Consider a child with high approach as peer support to other children who have social challenges.*

- A child with high approach is going to be confident about herself and her ability to make friends. Use her skills to support friends who may need friendship competency skill development through successful play inter-actions. You may need to direct how this is accomplished until you see successful relationships form.

- Pairing a child with high approach with a child who struggles with social skills (such as because of a special need) can benefit both children. The benefit to the child who has less-developed social skills will be positive interactions with a naturally outgoing child, building play and communica-tion skills. The child who is high in approach has the opportunity to learn empathy and respect for differences in her relationship with her peer.

- Before making an arrangement to pair two children where one is going to help build social skills for another, be sure they both agree to be play partners. It helps to support the play interaction with materials that the child who is less skilled has high interest in. For example, if the child likes airplanes, you could provide a bucket with airplane-themed activities for the two to engage in together.

## Story of Success

Aharon is easy to get along with in child care and never seems to mind when the schedule is changed and he has to wait for his favorite activity, which is playing outside on the climber. He has lots of friends who want to play with him, like doing follow-the-leader across the bars or down the slides. Sometimes he doesn't think about how high the slide is, and he has tried to jump when he slides halfway down. Not only is this against classroom rules, but it is also unsafe for Aharon. His teacher, Mr. Mike, decided that he and Aharon would practice some safety sliding. Mr. Mike made it like a safari. All the kids wore pretend safari safety gear, like helmets, and pretended that the slide was a tall tree in the jungle. He showed them how they needed to slide down one way to be safe and had them practice, like they were still in the jungle. Aharon still gets excited to go outside to play, but he remembers that he has to be safe to keep having fun.

## How Does a Child Express Withdrawal or Low Approach?

On the other side of approachability is the characteristic of withdrawal, or being slow to warm up. A child who is on the low side of approach and is high in withdrawal is going to be hesitant in new situations with new people and will pause before she tries something different until she feels more confident about it. She likes to know what is coming next, so surprises can result in challenging behaviors if she hasn't been made ready. Her reactions are based on her need for structure, routine, and sameness. A child with high withdrawal is looking for control, which is not always possible in the changing world of child care.

### Challenging Behaviors

Separation anxiety, while common for many toddlers, is greater for a child who has this temperament trait. He will also have a harder time being soothed when separated from his primary caregivers. This can make introducing a new activity center or a new program harder for a teacher. The approach to a new center needs to be planned so this child will slowly want to join in rather than resist it from the start.

A child with low approach may want to sit back and watch for a while before joining in. This gives him time to feel secure in what is happening and gain his bearings. He might even openly resist a change by refusing to participate or leave the center he is in if he doesn't like moving to a new room for art activities. A teacher may hear a lot of "No, no, no" from a toddler when he is asked to do something new or different.

Unexpected changes like a substitute teacher will be especially hard. It may take this child most of the day to warm up to someone other than his own teacher. Slowly approaching the child and matching his mood is more effective than trying to win him over with lots of enthusiasm that he doesn't share.

As discussed in chapter 2, goodness of fit is about the compatibility of a child's temperament traits, particularly dominant traits or his temperament type, with his interactions with people and the environment. When a temperament trait is challenging, like slow to warm, and adds up to an overall fearful temperament type, teachers and the child care program will need to make more adjustments. Many adaptations are part of what you are doing to meet diverse needs already, like intentionally using routines and consistent care practices. Others are more specific to this temperament type and may take tweaking to find the best way to reach a child who wants to be part of your program but may not know how he can securely reach out.

> Takima was in her grandmother's care while her parents worked for the first two and a half years of her life. She is now in a neighborhood family child care program where there is one infant and three preschoolers. While she has been coming here for four months, she still has a very hard time when her mother drops her off, clinging to her mother and crying. She holds tightly on to a small blankie that she is allowed to keep when she comes in, but she has to put it next to her backpack after breakfast snack. Sometimes she does not want to do that either.

## Positive Behaviors

For child care providers, there can be more challenges in working with a child who needs to hold back and wait until she feels more comfortable with a situation. However, there are positives too. On the plus side, a child who is slower to approach will tend to think before she acts. She is less likely than the high-approach child to rush in before knowing what to expect. More impulse control can prevent accidents and keep the child safer than one who moves first and then thinks about her actions.

Peers who share a slower approach disposition may prefer to be with a friend who isn't trying new things in her play or bringing a new play partner into a comfortable arrangement. A word of caution here, though: We want to be constantly observing and assessing children's interactions to ensure that all children are engaged and included with a wide variety of experiences in our programs.

## Effects on the Child's Relationships with Peers and Adults

This is a tough temperament trait for relationships with peers, because a child who is shier and less approachable may not seem as friendly until her friends get to know her. Even then, it is likely this child will have one or two friends she sticks closer to rather than a large circle of friends like a child who is highly adaptable and sociable.

There is no wrong or right to a child's disposition, but it can present barriers to social competence. Social competence can be seen as the capacity to initiate and maintain a satisfying and reciprocal relationship with another person. It's important that all children have some skills in initiating in order to start play or find common ground with a peer. Friendships can be hard for a child who is hesitant with new people or situations. A child who is withdrawing may not seek out friendships at first. She may wait for others to come to her, and because of her reticence, some children may choose to play with more approachable peers instead.

She may choose to engage in solitary play instead of group or cooperative play, losing some opportunities to gain social competencies. She may play alone by choice, or she may be afraid to approach a group that is already playing together.

She may have only one or two close peers she prefers to play with and thus may avoid large group activities. This means she misses opportunities to build friendships with people she doesn't know well. It isn't a negative to have close friends in child care, but we do want children to be part of a wide range of social experiences. We also want to avoid allowing cliques to form and exclude anyone.

Maintaining a friendship may be a bit easier than initiating for a child who has low approach, because she will probably stay true to a friendship she has made.

As a teacher, you may find it harder to build a relationship with a child who is high on withdrawal. We are more naturally drawn to a child who comes into the room full of energy and enthusiasm, happy to see us, instead of one who enters slowly, holding back, maybe even tearful. This approach to the world may be very different from your temperament as a teacher too. If you are more like this child, you will empathize with the way she hesitates when she comes into the classroom or when a new situation in child care arises and she withdraws. But if you tend toward high approach and high energy, you may struggle to find the positive lens through which to see this child who seems inflexible and resistant.

As you work with a child who is slow to warm, keep in mind that building a strong responsive relationship with her primary caregiver will help her be less anxious and insecure. For example, if you are going on a field trip to the museum, because she is unsure in new situations, she may cling to you on the bus and at the event. If you understand her temperament need to feel secure, you will help her with reassurances. When she arrives in the morning, she may not begin play right away but may want to sit quietly and wait for her favorite friend to get there. Giving her time in the morning to settle in may set a positive course for the rest of her day. If you introduce a new center activity, she could refuse to participate even though everyone else is doing it, until she watches and sees how it all works.

Behaviors can escalate into crying or screaming if a child becomes too overwhelmed by the change or the transition is too abrupt. This can disrupt the whole classroom and cause frustration to both teacher and child. She may use withdrawing behaviors like isolating herself or playing alone quietly. While all children need to be provided some quiet time if they seek it, withdrawing behaviors can be as troubling as aggression for children's social-emotional development if left unchecked.

> Kailani comes into the center quietly after she says goodbye to her mom. She puts her backpack away and sits down near the cubbies. Teacher notices she is there and gives her a couple of minutes to get ready to join in with the others. Then Teacher invites her to come over to group time and asks her to sit next to him.

## Effects on Play Skills and Other Development

Play for toddlers is often done side by side, watching but not necessarily interacting. As they grow a bit older, into their threes and fours, play takes on a more social role as skills progress. Play is important because language is influenced when children share and talk, particularly as imaginative play increases. We want all our children to be engaged in developmentally appropriate play because that is how they learn to expand their words, work together, and grow their imaginations. A child who withdraws from play because there are too many children or it is unfamiliar to her is missing some of the advantages of the early childhood play experience.

While teachers need to be aware of how much time a low-approach child might be spending alone or disengaged, there are also social-emotional benefits for a child who likes to hold back at times. For instance, we know that this child prefers what is familiar to something new, including what he migrates toward in dramatic play or other activity centers. The familiar play routine he uses, like preferring to dress like a doctor, can help him build on previous make-believe that extends and expands his imagination. Staying in one play pattern for a period of time can help a child feel mastery and accomplishment. Again, the teacher will want to observe him and make sure he is continuing to move forward in meeting developmental goals and milestones.

While play is an influence on much of a child's early development, other developmental domains can be hindered by a child who is slow to try new things or draws back rather than participates. Sometimes it can be hard to notice that a child is not participating in all the learning activities because she is so quiet and not making a fuss. If this is the case, we want to make sure she is not missing out on what we have designed as curriculum goals for our classroom. Specifically, encouraging her to play with new materials, like different kinds of building manipulatives, can increase sensory awareness and sensorimotor development. Participating in group games like Simon Says and Captain, May I? builds friendships as well as regulatory skills and language skills. Playing with peers in outside play increases motor development and imagination in making up games, running, and climbing. A child's learning and mastery in these skill sets is impacted negatively if she refuses to join in to new activities. Again, play is where and how children learn.

## Strategies to Meet the Needs of a Child Who Has Withdrawal or Low Approach

For the child whose temperament is closer to withdrawal or slow to warm up, people and situations that are new can cause anxiousness and fearfulness. Rather than embrace change, this child wants to run away from it. We can set up the environment so a child whose initial response is to hold back will feel secure enough to try new things:

### *Keep your schedule and programming as consistent as possible.*

- One way to achieve consistency for a child who is anxious about change is to have the same person greet him every morning. This starts off his day on a positive and secure note. It is a routine that internalizes for him a sense of security.

- Other consistent routines will help a child feel safe and secure so she will be able to approach more quickly and be more open to something new or varied. Routines include the way you begin each day with children, perhaps a common song in circle time, or the transition cues you use throughout the day. Routines include your schedule so a child knows that lunch always follows outside play.

- Use a visual picture schedule that shows your daily routine. It doesn't have to be complex, simply showing the activities in order of sequence through-out the day. Refer to the visual schedule frequently as you prep a child for the next event. Each time you refer to it, it reinforces a sense of security for her and builds on her biological regulatory system.

### *Avoid rushing a child who is low in approach.*

- Give her time to get familiar with a setting. If the child is new to your program, let her go at her own pace for the first few days. Don't expect her to make friends right away or jump into all of the activities. Let her explore and slowly take it all in. If it seems like she is not engaging after a few days, intervene by connecting her with a more approachable peer. Watch her play to ensure she has words to enter play with others when she is ready.

- This child is more likely to warm up when approached in a way that respects her temperament traits. When she arrives in the morning, wait to see her mood and match it with your own. If she is low-key, approach her with less energy than you might a child on the high end of approach.

### Consider letting him keep a favored transitional object from home to help him feel more secure.

- Give easy access to the object for the child, either letting him keep it by his side or leaving it in his cubby where he can go to it when he needs to. Because he is high in withdrawal, this may help him feel secure as he enters your program so that he will engage in play or with friends. Throughout the day, if something new or different happens, his transitional object is his anchor for security. This can be a preventative strategy to avoid tearful reactions or refusals to participate.

- You get to make your rules for how the transitional object is used by the child. If it is a blanket or stuffed animal, you might tell a child and his parents that it comes out for naps only, but he can go hold it when he needs to. It needs to work with your program, keeping in mind that it can add a sense of security and consistency for a child who tends to be fearful and slow to join.

- Be prepared to let all children know that in your program you strive to help everyone feel comfortable and safe. Tell them that some children need a blanket and some children don't, and both ways are okay. The important thing is that whatever each child needs, you are there to help them and support them.

### Encourage parents to have a goodbye ritual.

- A child who is low in approach and high in withdrawal may have a lot of difficulty at drop-off in the morning. Parents may be tempted to sneak out without saying goodbye to avoid the tears, but even if their child struggles with separation, encourage them to say goodbye and remind her that they will be back at the end of the day.

- When a parent disappears without saying goodbye, it can increase the child's fearfulness of separation and make it harder for her to seek out others as the new day begins.

- As the child gets older and has better understanding of emotional language, acknowledge her feelings with phrases like "I know it's hard to leave Daddy" as you quietly help redirect her to what is happening in the program.

*Promote emotional literacy.*

- Help a child practice words for feelings like "I'm afraid," "I'm worried," or other emotions that a child who doesn't feel comfortable with new situations or people might be feeling. Depending on his age, you could practice situations where he might use the phrases.

- Include books that teach words for feelings as part of your group time or one-on-one with this child. You can also use books about specific issues like separation, a new baby in the house, and other events that might cause a child to have more anxiety.

- Consider using *bibliotherapy*, which is making a small book with words and pictures specific to the child's worry and reading it with the child. It acknowledges the emotion and offers two or three tools for handling the emotion. You can use the book over and over with a child until she feels more secure.

- Let him know that all feelings are okay to express. Provide strategies to the child for what he can do with his big emotions, like worry or fear. For example, let him know that he can talk to Teacher or take a break.

*Make buddy buckets for a child more withdrawing and a child higher on approach to share.*

- Partnering the child who has more withdrawing behaviors with a more outgoing child can help her build social competencies and friendship skills one-on-one. Make sure both children want to participate.

- The buddy bucket has activities and toys that build on the interest of the child who is slow to warm, like a book on trains, a puzzle with a train, and a game that includes types of transportation.

- Use the buddy bucket to lead to other group play. You can use the interest items to help the child enter into large play by setting up a play situation in which you know the child will be engaged.

*Incorporate visual supports.*

- Visual supports include a picture schedule, posted rules, individual picture schedules, and labels on toy bins and posted directions for center activities. They include a picture or photo with the word that describes the picture.

- Visual supports will help a child who is slow to warm up to feel more secure when there are changes in the schedule. Using the visual supports with consistency is the key to their effectiveness with a child who feels insecure or is slow to approach new situations.

- If you know the schedule will be different because of a special event happening in the near future, talk about it ahead of time with this child and explain to him what will be happening so there are no surprises. Include any changes on the picture schedule for the week.

### Never cajole a child into being more socially active than she is comfortable being.

- While peer interactions are important and support social-emotional development, we want to honor the natural inclination of a child. A child who is low in approach is not going to become a social butterfly. You can help her feel secure in your setting and help her make and keep friends.

- Find positive ways to encourage involvement in your activities and projects with others by promoting shared interests.

- Look for ways to build her confidence so she will try new things. When she does something for the first time, build on that success with encouragement to try other things as well. Let her know she was successful.

### Encourage any efforts the child makes to try something new or enter a new play situation.

- Use positive encouragement and praise to reinforce the behavior. Be specific about what the child did, like "You were having a lot of fun with Jenny and Jacob in the art center with the new glitter paints."

- Use physical cues when a child is entering a new group to play, like a high five or thumbs-up.

### Create smaller groups so as not to overwhelm the child.

- Depending on your staffing and schedules, try to divide children into playgroups of three to four within an activity center that might normally be a larger group.

- Be available as a social support to help him enter the playgroup. He might need a prop to enter play, like a race car, or words to enter, like "I want to play with you" or "May I be the server?"

*Think of ways to structure solitary play that could segue into a group activity.*

- A child may find playing next to a group more comfortable before she enters into group play.

- Ensure that she has props to enter into the group when she is ready to play.

*Avoid labels for a child who is slow to warm up.*

- A child who holds back might be called the "shy" child by his teachers. Being shy can sometimes become a negative label if he is compared to more outgoing children or if the expectation is that he will always be shy.

- Be aware of actions or body language that might tell a child you think he could be more social or there is something wrong with his natural disposition. Even if you aren't directly saying, "Don't be so shy," your actions may be giving the child the impression that he needs to change.

## Story of Success

Franco, at age three, is an only child. When his mom enrolled him at Sunnyside Child Care Center, he was overwhelmed by all the children in his classroom and on the playground at one time. There was so much noise too. He would sit along the edge of the classroom and watch, rarely engaging with peers. Slowly he has gotten more accustomed to the children because he recognizes them and knows that some of the boys like the same block area that he does. His teacher sits next to him in the block area and hands him blocks while Timothy and Azad build too. They all three build a police station and then add cars and trucks.

# 8

# Intensity—Use Your Quiet Voice

Some children enter this life with great exuberance and noise. For them, nothing is done quietly! The key is to help them channel their energy, because the world needs movers and shakers!

Intensity as a temperament trait is the level of energy a child puts into his responses to the world around him. It is different from activity level, which refers to the overall need to be in motion (or not), while intensity refers to the volume or extent of the reaction. It is about his physical and emotional actions and reactions. When we say that temperament is about how a child is wired, intensity is easy to spot because it is through and through a child's whole system:

- how he walks and talks

- how he laughs and cries

- how he plays and fights

Intensity can be seen as passion or moderation, depending on the impact on a child's personality. You don't even need to turn around to see who is coming through your door if the child has high intensity, because you can hear him before he arrives. His arrival is bigger and louder than anyone else in his voice, his steps, and maybe even the slamming of the door! When we look at intensity as a temperament trait, we recognize characteristics along a spectrum of high intensity, low intensity, or somewhere in the middle.

A child with high intensity is often seen as having high highs and low lows. On the opposite end, a child with low intensity might sit quietly and take in what is going on around her without a lot of reaction or with no reaction at all. Even with infants, we see babies who squirm constantly and fuss a lot and those who will cuddle in and be content just to rest in the caregiver's arms.

It is the reaction to the event, whether positive or negative, that defines the intensity. Intensity can often override other temperament traits when it comes to a child's reactions and the resulting behaviors.

## How Does a Child Express High Intensity?

A child with high intensity might react to a happy event with loud laughter and jumping up and down. The same child might react to a sad situation by crying big "alligator" tears and dramatically throwing herself on the floor.

High intensity, coupled with other temperament traits like high distractibility and high activity level, means a child is in the feisty temperament type. As we have seen in previous chapters, each of these traits can result in challenging behaviors if the environment is not adapted in a way that supports impulse control and regulation skills. Teachers and children who have similar high-intensity personalities can often face challenging relationships. They may find themselves in a battle of wills at times, with neither one willing to back down because they are both having strong emotional reactions.

If a child has high intensity and his provider has low intensity, the adult may perceive the reaction of a child as extreme and begin to resent the child's behaviors. It can almost seem like his reactions are personal and that he is trying to push your buttons. For instance, if you have told a child in your program that he needs to stop stomping his feet when he walks inside, yet he continues to take loud steps, you might begin to think that he is doing that just to get under your skin. In fact, if he has high intensity as a dominant temperament trait, he probably isn't even aware of how loud he is walking. It is important to recognize intensity as a temperament trait so behavior can be seen through the lens of wiring and not as naughty or defiant. In this way, you can adopt strategies to teach the child more tools for impulse control to better regulate intensity.

> Daisy is six months old and is in the infant room of ABC Child Care. She tends to be a fussy infant, crying loudly when she needs attention from one of the infant teachers. She is harder to settle than the other infants in the room, usually taking longer to fall asleep at naptime. Her primary teacher is struggling to build a relationship with her because he isn't sure he knows the best way to respond to her needs.

### Challenging Behaviors

It's fair to say that intensity behaviors can exhaust caregivers in ways similar to high activity and high impulsivity. When we look at all nine temperament traits, high intensity may be one of the most difficult when it comes to your patience and ability to manage ups and downs over time.

A child who stomps instead of walks, who bangs his glass on the table instead of setting it down, who sings at the top of his lungs—all this can become too much at the end of a long day or week. Additionally, a child with high intensity may react strongly to even minor events. For instance, his response to a paper cut could sound like a major accident has occurred.

A child who screams his requests instead of asking can be difficult to handle for even the most seasoned teacher. Exuberance can be overwhelming to other children, especially those who are slower to warm. Loud laughter or bear hugs can be too much to handle for a child who tends to be reserved or likes to hold back before getting too involved.

Nothing this child does will be "small." If the child doesn't want to transition, his refusals will be loud. Physically, he will often use his whole body to express unhappiness by throwing himself down or jumping up and down. Sometimes the child with high intensity will go from happy to sad in a matter of seconds, and the emotional reaction will seem to be extreme based on the circumstances. This can upset the other children as well as frustrate the teacher.

While high-intensity behaviors may seem difficult to handle, remember above all that this is still only a child, reacting naturally with his body and emotions. Teachers will benefit from keeping a positive perspective. Again, we want to affirm high intensity as a natural part of who a child is. Sometimes it might be scary for the child, too, to have such a high level of emotions.

What children need from us is guidance on how to regulate those big feelings and big reactions. We also want to help children learn to control them. We can do this through the way we set up our environments to support regulation and impulse control, as well as guiding children to know when and where "big" reactions can be expressed most appropriately. The strategies at the end of this section will have more specific ideas for you as you work with high intensity behaviors.

## Positive Behaviors

If you are working with a child who has high intensity, some behaviors may challenge your positivity. But as with all traits that make up who children are, we can find ways to honor what makes them unique and special. We can also appreciate how different traits that present challenges in early childhood, including high intensity, will actually be strengths in many fields and careers later on. If we can set aside our own emotional reaction to the high-intensity behaviors of a child, we can see strengths too.

A child with high intensity will have a high-energy approach to life that can charge up the rest of the classroom. Sometimes we need to spice things up so children aren't doing the same things the same way every day. A child with high intensity tends to get noticed more and have her needs met more often. This can benefit the attached relationship this child has with adults because there are more interactions between them. The sheer magnitude of her energy can often bring adults and other children running to her to see what she has or wants or needs. She is a child who enjoys life with great enthusiasm, which can be contagious.

It's fun to have a child react with lots of gusto to our story time or the puppet show. Often this kind of energy is infectious and helps all the children get more animated and involved. You always know where you stand with this child! He will let you know if he loves something or hates it, and there is seldom an in-between. Intensity may be hard to handle at times, but it can also add a lot of flair to your program. Many teachers would rather have a child who shows a lot of emotions than a child who is hard to read or doesn't get involved.

## Effects on the Child's Relationships with Peers and Adults

High intensity as a dominant temperament trait presents some challenges to a child in making friendships work. Since relationships are a two-way street, it can be hard on the child on the receiving end of the intensity as well. The child with high intensity may not understand why a peer may regard his reactions as scary. He might think that everyone talks as loud as he does or that big reactions are the norm. Peers may shy away from a friend who screams when he gets upset or shouts when he is happy. If other children are quieter and more on the withdrawal side, a noisy, physical child might be upsetting because they don't respond in the same ways. If a friend does not know how a child with high intensity is going to react to different situations and thinks he is too unpredictable, she may begin to avoid that child and play elsewhere.

A child with high intensity may be bossy to peers and demand his own way. Other children may want a friend who is easier to get along with.

A child with high intensity can miss out on important early relationships that teach her how to play successfully, negotiate and problem solve, and share with peers. Those social competencies are important to ongoing social-emotional development and a positive view of self. A child with high intensity could begin to see herself as different but not know why for sure. She could begin to allow some of the negative attention she receives from peers to become part of how she sees herself. It could also make her frustrated or resentful and result in challenging behaviors against the peers who don't want to be around her.

For the early educator, working with a child who has high intensity as a dominant trait can hurt the ongoing attached relationship if the teacher is not aware of her own emotions about high intensity. As stated earlier in the chapter, some of this will depend on where she falls on the intensity spectrum in her own temperament. If she is high, she may understand the child better because of her own life experiences. Or, conversely, she may clash with the child in battles of will. If the provider is very low-key, she may find that the child slights her sensibilities in ways that are hard for her to manage. She may want to like the child but find herself struggling with frustration at him and her own negative perceptions. Either way, there will be challenges to building a successful relationship.

Adults who have a classroom with lots of children may find it difficult to manage the outbursts of one child with high intensity while keeping everyone else organized, on task, and feeling safe. It's easy to get pulled into power struggles if a provider is not careful to avoid the pitfalls. A child with high intensity will test a provider's patience. He may stomp his feet when he walks in your classroom, and when this stomping is repeated behavior, it can seem to be louder and bigger than it actually is. It can begin to feel like he is doing it on purpose to see what your reaction will be or simply to push your buttons.

A child with high intensity may react strongly to sensory experiences. For instance, if he does not like the fabric of a shirt or the way the tacos smell, he may react with screams of "no" or another physical reaction like throwing himself to the floor. This child may display greater dramatic reactions when he doesn't get his way or if he falls on the playground. Depending on a teacher's ability to find humor in situations, a child who throws himself to the ground and wails might be too much on some days.

It is crucial that child care teachers understand the temperament behind the behaviors. Children are not acting out just to get to us. They are acting on their natural dispositions to be a certain way, whether that is quiet, shy, persistent, or in this case, fully expressive. A child's experience in life is pretty short when you consider how many months or years she has under her belt! In that time, she has had to learn to navigate a complicated social construct called child care. Every child needs responsive adults to guide her in social-skill development, regulatory skills, and age-appropriate behaviors.

> When Lenny comes into his family child care program, he is so excited to see everyone that sometimes he forgets the rule about big hugs. He runs right up to the first friend he sees and wraps them in a bear hug. Sometimes they both fall over from the impact.

## Effects on Play Skills and Other Development

Children use play to build and establish relationships. Through play they connect, share toys as well as words, and begin to learn the complicated back-and-forth that creates a relationship. When one child plays with another, each begins to build some social expectations of the other. Toddlers sit next to each other and watch, even though they may be playing alone. Preschoolers begin to learn that they are expected to share, take turns, and help out peers. All of this grows with their developmental stage and skills.

If one child has "big" energy responses to the world around him, like spitting out a funny taste in his mouth or jumping up and down in line, peers may be discouraged from engaging in play with him. Children may retreat from the child who yells at them for using the wrong color block or who keeps knocking over the hospital they are building whenever he turns around.

A child who has been isolated by peers because of his unpredictability may continue to jeopardize his friendships because he doesn't know how else to respond. For example, he may escalate challenging behaviors to get attention from others. Rather than toning it down, he may ramp it up. His behaviors can become a cycle of high-intensity reactions, avoidance by others, isolation, frustration, and greater intensity of reaction, resulting in further avoidance and isolation. This cycle has to be broken by the adult. The child with high intensity needs tools to regulate his strong reactions. That is where guidance (chapter 2) is so important in the work we do by helping children be successful and providing a goodness of fit.

Children with high intensity tend to play with their whole bodies. This is a plus for physical development and gross-motor growth because they are using their proprioceptive and vestibular senses to the max! It brings a lot of sensory input into their joints and muscles. It also encourages mastery of physical milestones like climbing and jumping. But it can be risky for the child without proper monitoring.

A child who has high-intensity behaviors tends to throw her whole mind and body into action and activities. This can increase confidence in her abilities and build her sense of self-efficacy because she feels successful. This is a plus for her mastery of physical milestones as she experiences the world around her through her actions and reactions. She may be more coordinated than is typical for her age because of how she uses her body.

She may find herself struggling to calm herself down, especially if she is in a highly emotional state. While we would typically see other preschoolers learning impulse control, mastering self-regulation milestones may be a challenge for her.

Social-emotional development is impacted by high intensity in a child. As we have already seen in this chapter, making and keeping friends is hard when your emotions are unpredictable. Without peer support, friendship skills tend to lag.

We can all picture the child with high intensity. He can be a delight one minute and seem to become out of control with the flip of a switch. Our goal is to help him find more of a middle ground in the level of energy that he gives to a response and reaction. We are not going to change high intensity. It is wired into this child as a core part of who he is. But we can help him find and practice tools to regulate himself. High intensity can be an asset to him as he grows and develops if he also is able to control his impulses more effectively.

## Strategies to Meet the Needs of a Child Who Has High Intensity

A child who has high intensity as a dominant temperament trait will show big reactions to even minor events in child care. Here are some ways to help a child regulate emotions and behaviors:

***Help him read his own body's cues to understand his emotions and feelings.***

- Keeping in mind his developmental age and ability, he can start to learn how to regulate the amount of energy he uses in his responses. He has to understand what it means when he is using lots of energy or less energy in reaction to excitement or frustration or anger.

- One way to do this is to help him understand how his heart beats faster when he gets excited and slows down when he is calm. He can put his hand over his heart or feel his pulse. The goal is for him to calm his heartbeat down. You can practice this with an older toddler or preschooler.

- Teach him to breathe deeply three times or count to five to slow his breathing down while he feels his heartbeat. Give him lots of practice and encourage him in even small successes. When he calms himself, talk about how he feels in that moment and how he can calm himself the next time he starts to get revved up.

- Provide a rich emotional-literacy environment. Read books with him about feelings and help him describe his feelings after you read. Let him draw pictures of himself showing when he is angry or frustrated and talk about what he can do to make himself feel more relaxed, then draw a new picture of when he is calmer.

***Provide quiet spaces for a child to use when she starts to become overaroused.***

- Teach a child how to use the quiet space and explain why it can help her. Support her understanding of how to relax when she is taking a break.

- Make your own rules for your quiet space. You can decide if it includes books, visual supports, pillows, or other materials. Keep it as free from sensory experiences as possible so a child can truly calm herself.

- Help a child know that she decides when her body feels calm and relaxed enough to rejoin the group. However, this should not become a place to isolate oneself or withdraw from participation. Keep a watchful eye for children who might be overusing this space. It could indicate a red flag for something stressful or traumatic going on in the child's life.

- Never use a take-a-break space as punishment or a consequence for a behavior.

- Practice taking a break with the child so she knows how she feels when she might need to take a break. Help her understand what it feels like when she relaxes too.

### Be aware of your sensory environment.

- Because the child with high intensity has strong reactions to begin with, try to keep the environment less stimulating for sensory systems. Turn music down and dim lights when possible. Keep unnecessary scents and smells to a minimum. Use calming colors where possible instead of bright, stimulating primary colors.

- If you know that a child reacts more to noise, for instance, make sure that your quiet play areas are truly quiet places. Create centers that have quiet play to provide calming activities, and keep these areas near each other.

- When possible, keep your group activities smaller in number. The more that is going on around a high-intensity child, the more he is going to match the energy level.

### Build on her ability to be dramatic.

- Offer opportunities for plays and other creative outlets. Let her be the director of a dramatic play when age appropriate. Let an older child cowrite a play with friends and put it on for the class.

- For younger children and preschoolers, make sure your dramatic play area is full of rich sensory experiences and creative ideas. Dramatic play can be a place where she uses her high energy to express herself where louder and more boisterous behaviors are appropriate. This will help her feel successful about her own personality and skills.

- Let her be the story reader in circle group or give opportunities for her to act things out with others. Even a smaller child will enjoy this activity.

### Read a child's cues for overstimulation.

- Look for the signs he presents before he gets too excited. Are there environmental events or a particular transition, for instance, that trigger overintensity? How can you avoid or lessen the impact of the event?

- For instance, maybe he begins to get very excited when he sees the snack being put out for the morning break. Your strategy could be having him help you with the snack so he isn't waiting. In this way, you are using his energy in a positive way and at the same time helping him feel competent.

- Provide calming activities before a child reaches a point where he will be harder to calm. Offer to help him take deep breaths, or ask him, "How is your engine running? Is it a ten? Can we make it a seven?" and help him practice calming his "engine" down.

### Provide outlets so children can use their loud or "big" reactions in ways that are appropriate.

- In the morning, you can have everyone march around the classroom. Let her be the leader of the marching band. Children can use pretend instruments. Marching provides input into children's proprioceptive sense and can lessen the need later to seek stimulation by running or stomping.

- Provide many opportunities for singing and reading out loud with a dramatic voice. Consider contests for the most dramatic reading of a book.

- Provide gross-motor play daily and in many forms. Let a child with high intensity jump on a mini-trampoline or practice how high she can jump outside. Where running is allowed, let her have opportunities to use her energy.

### Provide many opportunities for physical play to use high energy.

- Similar to the strategies above, incorporate lots of action games like Freeze Tag; Red Light, Green Light; and Simon Says into the day to keep children moving and using vigor.

- Give time for as much outside play as possible. Consider making a sensory trail where you put sensory objects like shells, rocks, and bark on the path for children to explore with their feet. Have jumping contests. Show them how to stretch and then hold themselves still.

- Make balance beams using tape strips on the floor and let the children walk without stepping off. Let them practice being gymnasts with simple floor exercises such as rolling like a sausage.

### Avoid power struggles.

- Don't get pulled into arguing with the child when he is being overstimulated or is expressing strong feelings about an activity or situation. Sidestep the refusal by offering choices instead.

- For example, if the child says, "No, I won't come inside," then the provider can say, "Do you want to walk like an elephant or walk sideways?" Giving the child a choice that is not arguing about coming inside will often diffuse the power struggle.

- At cleanup time, instead of giving him the opportunity to refuse a request to clean up the mess, consider saying, "Do you want to pick up the blue blocks or the red blocks?" Then you help him by picking up the other color blocks.

- Consider ways you can problem solve together before it becomes a struggle. If you know that a child is going to resist something, talk about it before it happens. Ask what you can both do to make the situation work. Avoid using the word *no* yourself, but instead say, "Yes, you can go to the art center as soon as the blocks are put away."

- Change the way you ask for something. For example, instead of asking a child to wait, ask him to be the one who watches over the line to keep everyone safe. Reframing the request can sometimes change the way the child perceives it. Help him feel like he is part of the solution.

### Give the child other ways to feel powerful and successful.

- Consider making her the leader of the group going outside when she says she isn't going to move from the art room. Can she help you get the others ready to go in some way? Make a job for her to help the transition work.

- Ask her for help. It might be helping you empty the garbage cans or move a table (even if it doesn't need to be moved very far). Enlist her energies to do something that she can see makes a difference.

- Validate her feelings. What does she need from you? Ask her how she is feeling. Name the feeling with her and talk about ways you can help her with that feeling.

### Take care of yourself.

- A child with high intensity can take a lot of energy from you. Make sure you are not being pulled into struggles with him that result in everyone feeling frustrated, including yourself. Learn to recognize the cues for possible power struggles so you can stop them before they begin.

- If you are beginning to have negative feelings about this child, remember to use the lens of temperament. Examine your own temperament when it comes to intensity. Realize he isn't doing this to ruin your day but rather needs guidance to control his impulses and behaviors.

- Use proactive self-care strategies for yourself. Engage in whatever works to make you feel organized and calmer, and make sure you do not put it off. You need to be wholly well and feel successful to help a child feel successful.

## Story of Success

Nina was highly sensitive to the world around her, even as an infant. She squirmed a lot when she was little and was hard to settle, according to her grandma who brings her to Ms. DeEtta's family child care home. She is now thirty months old and still reacts strongly when Ms. DeEtta says it is naptime. Nina doesn't like to lie on the mat because it feels scratchy, and she doesn't like to stop playing either. Sometimes she screams at Ms. DeEtta and says, "No, I won't," but Ms. DeEtta says that after nap there is snack. Nina likes the vanilla wafers, and so sometimes she lies down without saying anything.

# How Does a Child Express Low Intensity?

The differences in temperament traits from high to low is fascinating to anyone who studies children's innate personalities. While high intensity would support the feisty or harder-to-handle temperament type, low intensity is more likely to be seen in a child who is flexible because it fits more with adaptability and low sensitivity. Depending on how strong the lack of reaction is, a child could also be considered slow to warm up or fearful if he is also low on approach. The child with low intensity will sometimes present challenging behaviors, though in a very different way than a high-intensity child. As with all temperament traits from high to low, there are also benefits to each child's unique temperament.

## Challenging Behaviors

Low intensity might seem like it would be easier to deal with than other traits because you will not usually see aggressive behaviors like hitting or spitting or loud emotional outbursts. But because a child is harder to read and may not tell you what is bothering her, you could tend to overlook what she needs and give more attention to the child who is demanding your attention. A child with low intensity may show little or no typical reaction to the events going on around her or may give no indication of what emotions she is experiencing. She may feel scared or insecure but cover it up with withdrawing behaviors that the teacher doesn't notice because they are subtle and quiet.

Sometimes it may be hard to know if this child is engaged in an activity because of his lack of energy or emotion. You may feel that he doesn't like something because his smile is slight or he doesn't laugh with the same enthusiasm as his peers. A child could actually be missing out on gaining the emotional-literacy skills of other children in the program because he keeps feelings inside. There may be less back-and-forth communication in emotional language with peers.

When upset, a child who has low intensity may sit quietly in the corner. An adult might not notice his distress unless they are particularly tuned in to the child's emotions. A child with low reactions may not let you know that he is being bullied by a peer or left out by others. Left unchecked, this could lead to feelings of isolation for the child and further withdrawal. Not only does this create a barrier for his continued learning through peer engagement, but it also can promote a lower sense of worth. Ensuring that all children feel included means being aware of all the differences in children and their approach to the world around them.

> Sasha was a quiet baby who barely fussed when she was hungry or sleepy. Now that she is ready for the older toddler room at her child care center, her teacher knows that Sasha will likely not fuss when she needs a snack or diaper change. Her teacher is trying to stay tuned in to Sasha's subtle cues that something is wrong so she can build a responsive and attached relationship with her.

## Positive Behaviors

Low intensity usually means a child is flexible and easy to get along with. The child has less of a reaction to what is going on around him, and if it is coupled with adaptability and positive mood, this child is probably a pleasure to have in a classroom. For example, a child who has low intensity will be less likely to overreact to changes in his world. He may fuss a bit instead of using a more challenging behavior when it is time to change a preferred activity.

Additionally, this child will be less demanding of the caregiver's attention. He will tend to sit back rather than be the first to ask for something. He will also be unlikely to show either pleasure or displeasure with a situation.

Generally, he will have greater toleration for sensory stimulation in the environment than a child with high intensity. This includes the sounds and smells of the setting as well as his own socks, shirts, carpet square, and so forth. He will have less reaction to changes and transitions. Some of the positives offered here can also be challenges because teachers have to work harder to know what he is thinking or feeling. We want all children to feel like they belong in our programs and feel safe enough to tell us when someone is teasing them or not sharing. A child with low intensity may need extra observation to make sure he is standing up for himself and expressing himself to us and peers when he needs to.

## Effects on the Child's Relationships with Peers and Adults

The effect of low intensity on a child's relationships with both adults and peers will vary depending on other temperament traits she may have. If she tends to be more withdrawn as well, it will be harder to build a relationship with her without intentionality and focus. Teachers will need to approach slowly and closely observe her mood. If she has low intensity combined with a positive mood and regularity, she will be easier to approach and will offer to engage with everyone. Knowing each child's whole temperament, with emphasis on the influence of dominant traits, gives you a better picture of what she needs in a behavior guidance plan.

As much as high intensity can get in the way of building a relationship between child and adult, the same may be true of children with low intensity. Adults may not be as drawn to a child who is less expressive of his needs. You have to work harder to know what he wants or needs from you. Because his reactions are less intense, a child may not get as much attention from adults as a louder, more demanding peer. He still needs teacher attention, however, and may not know how to express his needs.

A child with high intensity may be demanding, but he also brings a lot of energy and excitement to a room! A child who has low intensity does not encourage others to get involved in a new game or try an activity in a more creative way. A child with low intensity will not show providers the same enthusiasm for a new food or a special event like going to the zoo. We might look for a display of happiness and eagerness that could deflate us a bit if we expect too much from this child.

While it may take longer to understand the emotional needs of the child with low intensity, once we know his cues we can build a successful and reciprocal relationship with him. Much of what can be a barrier for adults in building effective relationships with a child with low intensity will also get in the way of peer-to-peer relationships. We can facilitate social interactions in our programs by being aware of the relationship skills and gaps of a child with low intensity.

We discussed earlier how children might avoid a child who is unpredictable with high intensity, but peers might leave out a child who doesn't engage or show much response to them. It will be difficult for her to make friends if she is left to solitary play. She also won't show a lot of laughter and enthusiasm, which could mean peers would be more drawn to the friends who are high on approach instead of her. She may avoid physical play and make it harder for other children to engage with her because she prefers more sedentary play.

Conversely, children could also be drawn to her because she is easy to get along with and doesn't make demands. Once she is invited to play, she will go with the flow of the game without making changes or insisting on her way. She will not be overreactive in her emotions with other children, making her a more pleasant playmate. A child low in intensity will not express preferences for a toy or game, so sharing with her is easier.

A child with low intensity has challenges within himself to making and keeping friends. The biggest challenge is that he may avoid what makes him uncomfortable, like other children who seem louder or more physical than he is. Keeping him engaged with his interests and expanding those interests to include other children will keep him in the mix and not on the fringe of the early childhood setting.

## Effects on Play Skills and Other Development

A child with low intensity will either be a preferred play partner among her peers, or she will be left out. This depends a great deal on how tuned in the adults are at pulling her into activities and encouraging play partnerships with other children. If she tends to be left alone because she is quiet and doesn't demand attention, she will lose some key benefits. She won't gain skills from play like exploration, creativity, and experimentation. A child with low intensity tends toward less responsive interactions to begin with and needs help engaging in order to benefit from play partnerships.

A child who sits on the sidelines is not using physical movement to become better coordinated and develop gross-motor skills. A child with low intensity may avoid rough-and-tumble play altogether, so drawing her into active play will encourage motor skills.

A child with low intensity who avoids getting involved is not going to use her imagination in dramatic play or in games with peers. Games are important for learning rules that help support regulatory skills as well as for changing the rules, and thereby encouraging creativity and stimulating cognitive development. Dramatic and imaginative play support language development and cognitive skills that will be impacted if a child is not encouraged to participate.

Low intensity can mean a child does not follow through in an activity if someone interrupts his play by taking away a toy or not giving him the glue stick. Because he does not tend to react strongly, he may just move on to something else. Finishing a task gives a child a sense of success and self-efficacy, which are important to ongoing social-emotional growth and positive self-worth. On the other hand, a child who has minor reactions to mishaps in play or even aggressiveness from peers may find himself a sought-out play partner because of his easygoing manner.

As you can see, low intensity in a child as a dominant temperament trait can be positive or challenging depending on the interventions that are made on the child's behalf to engage and include him. Below we will begin looking at strategies for a child with low intensity to ensure he can be more successfully supported in your child care program.

## Strategies to Meet the Needs of a Child Who Has Low Intensity

A provider who works with a child who is mild in his reactions must be mindful of the child's level of engagement and be watchful for withdrawing behaviors. A child who is slow to react or subdued in reaction may benefit from the following strategies:

### *Learn her subtle cues for feelings and emotions.*

- Because a child with low intensity does not show a high level of emotion, her signs of sadness or unhappiness may not look the same as a typical peer who might cry or have a gloomy face. However, it is important to respond to her needs if something has upset her. Knowing how she expresses emotions like sadness or frustration will help you give her the most effective support.

- Use books on specific emotions to help a child learn words for feelings. Ask her what sad looks like to her so you know what to look for. Practice emotions with her, using feelings charts or feelings cue cards. Create your own books using bibliotherapy that are specific to her feelings and the strategies you create together.

- Don't expect her to show you emotional outbursts or wider degrees of feelings even though you have talked about her feelings. Her temperament will remain fairly stable, but you still want her to have words to express herself. Never discourage a child's lack of expression of feeling by comparing her to others, for instance, "Everyone else looks so happy to have birthday cake today." Remember she is uniquely built the way she is.

### *Look for signs of internalizing behaviors.*

- Internalizing behaviors are behaviors that are inward focused and include isolating oneself, withdrawing, or not communicating. If you know that a child tends toward low intensity, you can be mindful of these behaviors to ensure he does not tune out of your program.

- You may recognize internalizing behaviors in a child who doesn't stand up for himself when someone takes his toy or when he is bullied by peers. He may also be left out or not included in a child care clique. He may become more withdrawn by these situations.

- Help him learn and practice words to express his feelings, like "I don't like it when you make fun of my name," or "Teacher says everyone gets a turn."

- Ensure that your classroom is inclusive in practice as well as philosophy. Developing an intentional child care community fosters a sense of belonging for everyone and discourages children from leaving others out. A community is built by giving everyone jobs, showcasing family rituals and photos, and holding class meetings when the children are old enough. Verbalize that everyone belongs in your classroom.

### Encourage engagement and involvement by building on the child's interest areas.

- If a child likes dogs, for example, use circle time to talk about pets. Extend other activities into shared reading of children's own stories about their pet dogs. Play a bingo game that children create by cutting out pictures of dogs and gluing them on a lotto page.

- Involve peers who have strong friendship skills in play partnerships with a child who is hesitant to join play. Pair up a child who is high on approach with a child who is low on intensity with a buddy bucket (page 111) to encourage social-skill development and friendships.

### Talk frequently to this child about how he is feeling.

- Offer encouragement when he expresses himself to you or others by using phrases like "You were laughing at the face that Jason made! Wasn't he funny?"

- Validate his feelings, no matter how low-key his expression of them. He is wired to be quieter and more subdued. Help him know that how he expresses himself is okay.

***Help her learn to be more assertive with peers.***

- Because she may be less likely to complain or fuss, other children may take advantage of her withdrawing nature by not sharing with her or not giving her a turn. While you are on the watch for this, she also needs to learn skills to stand up for herself.

- Practice phrases she can use with peers, like "It's my turn" or "I want that now." Also practice talking to an adult if someone is bullying her by taking something away or leaving her out on purpose.

## Story of Success

Santiago is twelve months old and enrolled at Great Beginnings Child Care Center. He is very low-key, expressing his needs for a diaper change or feeding with only a quiet cry. He rarely fusses if he does not need anything. The assistant teacher in the room, Ms. Wudan, talked to the lead teacher, Mr. Johnson, to ask if there is anything more she should be doing to provide responsive caregiving, an important value of their center. Mr. Johnson decided that they need to anticipate Santiago's needs more, in advance of signals he might give. So Ms. Wudan is making sure she holds and talks to him frequently throughout the day. In fact, she is becoming more tuned in to all the moods of each infant in her classroom. She feels more confident that she is providing the nurturance that each child needs, from the fussiest to the most serene.

# 9

## Regularity—How Does My Engine Run?

Justin says, "I don't want to go to lunch yet. I'm not hungry at all, and I don't want to eat." Meanwhile Jessica says, "It's snacktime on the picture schedule, but teacher isn't putting out crackers yet. I am so hungry, I don't think I can wait any longer. What is taking so long?"

Children come into child care programs with their own unique cycles of hunger, sleepiness, and playfulness. Regularity as a temperament trait refers to the biological and emotional rhythm of a child. It includes these things:

- eating

- sleeping

- elimination

- expression of feelings

Regularity can be predictable or unpredictable, depending on whether a child has high or low regularity. As with all temperament traits, the environment and genetics play important roles in a child's ongoing ability to regulate herself. For instance, a baby who is well regulated from birth may have consistent sleep patterns sooner than a baby with low regularity. We all know of the infant who doesn't know her night from day during the first weeks of sleeping, keeping her parents up much of the night. If the environment is particularly unsettling, noisy, or chaotic, it can also interfere with the child's natural ability to balance wake and sleep.

*Biological regularity* is about how often and recurrently a child will eat, sleep, and toilet. In young children, biological regularity is a work in progress. A child needs a consistent environment to become well regulated, even when he is born with high regularity. Some infants will have regular napping and sleeping habits from the start, but most develop a sleep rhythm based on an internal clock as well as environmental and caregiving influences.

For the child who has low regularity, the environment builds a pattern that can be internalized over time. This will support her in becoming better regulated, though she will not be well regulated the way a child who is high on this temperament trait will be.

*Emotional regularity* refers to how balanced a child's moods and feelings are. The two types of regulation are seen here as one temperament trait. We will look at both parts of regularity since both biology and emotions will affect the behaviors of a child in the child care setting.

The more a child follows a routine, the more consistent she will become in her needs for napping and eating. Routines build biological regularity, which in turn supports emotional regularity. A child's understanding of his own body and how it feels when he is hungry or tired also helps him begin to regulate his feelings. Biology and emotions are wrapped up together in the process of regulation and self-regulation.

As she develops greater cognitive and language skills, she can learn to read her body. She can express when she needs to take a break before becoming upset or overstimulated, or she can use words to talk about how she is feeling.

Emotional regulation means a child can respond to the ongoing demands around her with a range of emotions that are appropriate reactions or delay her reactions. A child low on regularity may find it hard to delay emotional reactions or use the appropriate behavioral reaction. For instance, if she wants the toy that someone else has, she may bite her friend to get the toy rather than waiting for a turn. A child high on regularity can make that pause between a thought (I want to play with your toy) and the action (I will wait for my turn with the toy).

Carrie is three and has a hard time controlling her emotions. She gets angry fast when a friend doesn't give her what she asks for, and sometimes she strikes out by pushing that friend. Some of her friends said they don't want to play with her, which makes her even angrier, but she doesn't know why for sure.

## How Does a Child Express High Regularity?

High regularity, like high adaptability or high approach, is a temperament trait that rarely causes a provider difficulties. A child with high regularity will be very predictable in her behaviors and will adapt easily to a regular schedule in child care. High regularity tends to put a child in the flexible temperament style.

Because child care programs have schedules with multiple transitions a day, a child who likes to follow a schedule and a routine will not worry about what is coming.

## Challenging Behaviors

There can be some difficulties with a child who is highly regulated, though, if unexpected disruptions to his normal pattern have occurred and his needs for routine are not being met.

If the daily calendar changes, it can throw off the child who is used to one schedule and whose body relies on that schedule. For instance, if he is used to always eating lunch at eleven thirty and lunch is moved later by thirty minutes, he may have difficulty waiting that extra half hour. You may see highly regulated children have difficulties adjusting sleep patterns with Daylight Saving Time, whether infants or preschoolers. Working with parents to adjust bedtime gradually up to the time change can help alleviate behaviors that come from poor sleep.

A child who likes a set schedule may find having vacations or holidays from child care difficult. You may see some challenging behaviors as a child anticipates the changes coming up or when she returns after a vacation and has to settle in again to a different routine from home or vacation.

A child with a pattern of high regularity will tend to be hungry or sleepy at the same times each day and may be challenged if her needs are not met on time. For instance, if napping is delayed because a field trip runs long, this child may have trouble soothing herself when everyone lies down for nap later in the afternoon.

High regularity can also mean rigidity. This can lead to behavior challenges when a child wants a pattern to be exactly the same or to fit a routine he is used to. When there is change in some way, the child may feel out of sync with the world around him. This discomfort can lead the child to use a challenging behavior to let you know that he doesn't like the changes to his routine and wants it to go back to what he is used to. Strategies for a child who needs a set pattern will follow at the end of this section.

## Positive Behaviors

Very few accommodations have to be made to fit the needs of a child who is well regulated in the child care program. A child with high regularity will follow the routines a teacher has set up and will actually prefer the rhythm of consistent practices. This is in contrast to a child with low regularity who has difficulty following routines based on her biological timetable.

A preschooler with high regularity will tend to want to be more organized. You may find that this child picks up and puts away things without a lot of prompting. She may enjoy sorting some of the play materials according to size or shape.

She will fall into new routines easier as well, so if you are moving a child from the toddler to preschool room, she will adapt to changes in the schedule much sooner. Another positive comes when it is time to toilet train, because her elimination is regular. She will probably be hungry when it is time for lunch and will eat it up!

Once you know her schedule for eating, sleeping, and elimination, you can tweak your schedule to ensure that she gets what she needs when her body needs it. She can help other children who may struggle more than she does with transitions by being a stabilizing and positive force as you promote routines and schedules.

## Effects on the Child's Relationships with Peers and Adults

High regularity and the need for routine can be a plus and a challenge when it comes to a child's relationships with her friends. It will be influenced by the dominant temperament traits of the peers she interacts with as well as whether her environment provides a goodness of fit. If a child who has high regularity plays with peers who also have high regularity and high adaptability, they should all get along well because they like following the daily schedule and adapt well to transitioning when it is time to move. On the other hand, peers who are low on regularity may be frustrated with a friend who likes a routine and structure for doing things. They may want to eat when he doesn't or go outside when it isn't on the schedule. They may find their friend somewhat inflexible and not as much fun as a peer who likes to mix it up.

If the child care setting is not consistent, a child with high regularity will struggle finding a sense of balance and well-being. He may become resistant to all the fluctuations in his routine and refuse to eat if it is too early or go outside if he thinks it is time to do art.

Typically, a child with high regularity will be easy to get along with because her emotions and behaviors are well regulated. Volatility would be unusual in her reactions to a peer because she has a fairly predictable pattern of interaction with others.

Teachers and caregivers will find a child with high regularity to be typically in the flexible temperament type, especially if he is also adaptable and has low intensity and low sensitivity. He is fairly easy to get along with and doesn't make much of a fuss as long as the routine is consistent. His nature depends on a structured and predictable schedule, and challenges may come when the setting is disorganized or disrupted.

A child with high regularity could have difficulty when the teacher introduces a new activity into the schedule that changes lunchtime or a favorite playtime. As with any child, he could use a challenging behavior if he feels out of sorts because the routine has been interrupted.

If the child care provider is low in regularity, it may be challenging for her to meet the needs of a child whom you can almost set a clock by when she wants to eat or go to the bathroom. The teacher may struggle with routines she has not had in place before and not understand why the child is so upset by changes.

For the most part, high regularity will mean a child has an easy and flexible temperament and will not produce a lot of challenging behaviors as long as the environment has consistent routines. Strategies to support this child mainly center around building a consistent structure for what happens each day. In this way, the child's biological need to be regulated is strengthened so she can be present and ready to learn.

Molly is six months old and has been very regular since early infancy. Early on she was eating and sleeping on a schedule, which delighted her mom and dad. Now that she is in child care, her teacher has noticed that she needs to eat on the right schedule or she becomes more and more upset and may refuse to eat at all until she can be soothed again.

## Effects on Play Skills and Other Development

A child who has high regularity will find playing with others easy because he doesn't get stuck in one area or one type of play. Once he is familiar with a child care schedule, he will move to the next activity because he likes to keep a routine. If art follows snack, he will go to art and then transition to outside play because that is what comes next. This is not to say that any child will not experience disagreements with friends over a favorite toy or be tired and grumpy some days, but in general he will be a flexible play partner.

He will tend to transition well from play area to play area when he is comfortable with the routine. He gains the benefits of play with peers because he is a positive play partner. Regularity does not mean he doesn't play creatively with toys or games. Because he is secure in the setting, he is flexible in how things are done as long as the schedule is followed.

Play builds confidence, dexterity, and language and cognitive skills through creating and exploring. Because a child with high regularity will like to play in a variety of settings and in different ways, she develops strong skills through play. Even when a game or an activity changes, she will adapt to the change as it becomes the routine for her. She internalizes habits and rules easily.

The minus here would be that if a child does not have the sense of security that comes from a consistent schedule and routine in child care, she may not feel that flexibility to roll with the changes. She may be anxious because her need for regularity is not being met and she does not know what to expect next. This will upset a child who needs reliability.

A child with high regularity may have some difficulty continuing in play if her body says it is time for lunch and the schedule is off that day or a program does not run a tight schedule of activities including mealtime.

Other development for a child with high regularity will be much like his approach to play skills. He will tend to stick to a task or activity because it is part of the routine of the day, so learning takes place when engagement takes place. A child who has high regularity and is able to keep to her body's schedule should be able to participate in projects, games, and activities without needing to use challenging behaviors to have her needs met. You can introduce new activities to this child and he will adjust well once he knows the structure of them. For instance, if you decide to start a new project about numbers and you use circle time and craft time to teach and practice the concepts, he will likely be eager to learn because it is still within his routine.

High regularity can be an asset to a child because it means she has a regular sleep pattern, making her rested when she comes to your program physically and emotionally ready to learn. She eats on a schedule, so if the meals have been provided to her, she isn't going to act out because she is hungry. She comes to your program biologically organized to be successful as long as her needs get met.

## Strategies to Meet the Needs of a Child Who Has High Regularity

For a child who keeps a regular and consistent pattern of eating, sleeping, and going to the bathroom, you can support her through the following strategies:

### Use a visual picture schedule.

- Using a visual picture schedule supports a child's need to know what is coming next. It helps assure him that lunch is after outside play and nothing has changed.

- A visual picture schedule that you refer to throughout the day will help prevent anxiety for a child who needs to follow a routine and needs to know what is happening next. He may only need to look at it once in a while to know he is secure and then be able to play without worries.

*Prepare this child for changes to routine as much as possible.*

- Changes in daily schedule can be a challenge for a child with high regularity, so let her know what is happening. Make a plan for the changes with the child.

- For example, if a teacher is going to be on maternity leave, talk about why she is leaving and who will take her place. Give the child strategies for what to do if she gets worried or anxious, such as talking to the director. Consider using bibliotherapy, creating a book about the situation and letting the child read it with you as often as she needs to in order to feel comfortable. Include strategies in the book that the child can practice.

- Minimize change as much as possible by thinking ahead. If you know a fire drill is coming on Tuesday, talk about it ahead of time. Put it on the picture schedule.

- If you know lunch is off schedule or delayed, offer a snack to stave off hunger pangs as well as challenging behaviors. A child who needs to eat at the same time every day could react with angry behaviors toward you or her peers if she doesn't get her biological need met. By being proactive you can prevent many challenges.

*Add some flexibility within a routine to help a child develop greater adaptive skills.*

- Have a child practice short waits as long as it does not cause frustration. For example, say, "Let's count to three before snack. One, two, three—here is your orange slice! What a good wait!"

- Talk about how he feels when changes to the schedule occur. Help him with words if he is still learning words for feelings. Problem solve together on ways to adapt to any changes. Help him find solutions.

*Be patient!*

- She may seem rigid at times, but remember that this is how she is wired naturally. You won't change her from being a child who likes a routine, but you can help her learn many coping skills for adjusting to waits or variations in a schedule.

- Help her as she gains more flexibility in adapting to variations in routines. Learning more adaptive skills may be a slow process. The more consistent your program, the more likely she will feel safe enough to take changes in stride.

- Remember that she is reacting to her biology. As she grows, she will become more flexible and more able to wait, but she needs a lot of time to practice!

- Recognize your own temperament when it comes to regularity. If it is not a match with this child, be aware of how you might clash, and work to ensure that neither of you ends up feeling frustrated.

### Story of Success

Bianca is three years old and goes to her neighborhood family child care program. She has a lot of energy and curiosity, so child care is always an adventure for her. Her child care provider, Ms. Yolanda, uses a visual picture schedule that is the same for each day, and she goes through it at morning meeting with the preschoolers in her program. She has a red arrow that she moves during the day to show what activity they have just begun; Bianca sometimes gets to be the one who moves the arrow. Bianca loves to know what is coming next. If it is snacktime and Ms. Yolanda is busy with the two toddlers, Bianca will say, "Ms. Yolanda, it's time for crackers!" Ms. Yolanda says, "Yes, you are right; it says so right on our schedule! It will be ready in just a jiffy." Bianca is learning patience, as much a three-year-old can muster.

## How Does a Child Express Low Regularity?

Low regularity as a temperament trait is going to have more implications for a child and his behavior than high regularity. If matched with high intensity, high distractibility, or high sensitivity, low regularity or irregular temperaments will mean a child is in the feisty or active temperament type. As mentioned in chapter 1, this type comprises about ten percent of all children, but they can be a vocal group! Low regularity means the child's biological clock doesn't set a very regular schedule for eating, sleeping, or eliminating. It also can impact emotional regularity, closely related to mood (see chapter 11).

### Challenging Behaviors

Low regularity is often a challenge for providers. If you have an infant who doesn't want to eat on any kind of schedule or for whom you cannot figure out a napping pattern, both you and the baby will be frustrated. The same infant grows into a toddler who doesn't want to nap with the rest of the group and then a preschooler who isn't hungry at lunch but acts out an hour later because that is when she is hungry and crabby.

In child care, we rely on scheduled events like lunch and nap because we know routines support children's physical, social, and emotional development. But it can be hard for a child who has an irregular pattern of biological needs to eat or nap at specific times in child care. A child's body rhythm can be random, making any type of routine hard to follow. Being forced to follow a schedule can result in resisting behaviors because it feels contrary to the child's natural rhythm.

You might see a child use fight or flight behaviors because she doesn't want to change right now. She may refuse to move or use aggression against the teacher if her body is telling her she doesn't want to go to the bathroom, for instance. Disruptive behaviors can occur if a child didn't sleep the night before and comes to the program tired. She may hit or bite her friend, and you won't know the reason for the aggression unless a parent tells you she had a restless night.

If she wasn't hungry at home and didn't eat breakfast but is hungry when she gets to your program, until she is old enough to ask for food, she may use challenging behaviors to tell you she is uncomfortable. She may cry or whine until snack is offered. A child who does not have regular elimination patterns may take longer to potty train.

When a child has low regulation, having to follow a schedule will be difficult without thoughtful guidance on the part of the teacher. For instance, a child may resist moving to naptime if he is not sleepy yet or may have a hard time settling down if an adult is not coregulating with him. If he is tired from lack of sleep, it will be difficult to move on to a new play activity that requires more energy or even simply a change. Challenging behaviors can result when the child is seeking or avoiding sleep or food.

Remember that children will develop skills that help them regulate their own bodies and emotions as they mature, but they need our help in getting there. A child needs tools for regulation and lots of time to practice them.

## Positive Behaviors

As a teacher, you can build on a child's behaviors that stem from his irregularity to reach more positive outcomes. A child who doesn't need a fixed routine will be more flexible. If you have last-minute changes to the schedule, he isn't as likely to be upset with an alteration to the day. He will tend to be more spontaneous because he isn't as concerned with what is coming next. This can be fun for you and the other children.

Depending on other temperament traits, he won't necessarily be fussy if snack is late or he isn't the first one to sit down for lunch. However, a child who is low on regularity may be hungry at other times, so keeping a snack bowl out all the time will alleviate challenges that might erupt from a hungry child.

## Effects on the Child's Relationships with Peers and Adults

A child with low regularity who balks at a schedule when it doesn't match her own biological needs may find herself at odds with peers who are better regulated. If she is also higher on sensitivity and intensity, she can be more difficult to get along with. Behaviors could include these:

- aggression when she is tired but it isn't naptime

- crying when she is hungry or pouting when she doesn't want to quit playing to go eat

- hitting because she doesn't think a friend is responding to what she needs

When a child does not have a strong inner routine, she is apt to feel less grounded and more insecure. This can lead to behaviors that disengage her from peers or cause her to fight with playmates because she isn't connected to them. When a child bites or spits on another child, we look at the possible function for the behavior, or the "why" of it. If we know a child is irregular in her own biological or emotional regulation, we can intervene with strategies to help build more regulation. These strategies will be included at the end of this chapter.

Low regularity can cause tension between teacher and child if the teacher is particularly regimented in her own biological schedule and lacks flexibility herself. A child who does not eat breakfast at home but is hungry just after arrival at child care may seem disruptive to circle time, for instance. It takes an understanding of this child's temperament to accommodate his need for small snacks throughout the day while still maintaining the schedule.

All children need routines to support ongoing social-emotional development. Routines and schedules give a child a sense of safety and security so he can build strong attachments with his primary caregivers. Low regularity puts a child's relationships at risk if adults do not intervene with tools for building more regularity. A child with low regularity will not become a biologically well-regulated preschooler, but he can become more aware of his own body and its needs so he can ask for help.

## Effects on Play Skills and Other Development

A child with low regularity may have some struggles in playing with others because her own biological clock doesn't match the schedule of activities in the child care program. Her ability to learn through play will be impeded if she can't be part of predictable programming. Child care providers need to be aware of how the child's temperament is influencing her behaviors and learning. For example, if a child isn't sure she will get what her body needs, she may not be able to get into a regular pattern of play with others. Also, if she is hungry during art but can see on the picture schedule that lunch is coming next, she may have trouble engaging in her project. A child can't learn if she isn't participating.

Whether it is time for stories or math concepts, if a child's biology is saying, "This is the time of day when I need to sleep, but I can't take a nap yet," she isn't going to be listening or learning. If a child has an irregular sleep pattern at home, it can affect her mood at child care. If she arrives tired, she may find it harder to navigate the social environment of child care and control her impulses. She might use tears to get out of an activity or to get her way with a friend. Helping her gain more predictability by understanding her body will help her be more ready to learn. Providing what she needs at different times of the day, like keeping pretzels on the counter for a snack between meals, can help her stay alert and involved.

The child care routine is a positive intervention tool for all temperament types for preventing challenging behaviors before they occur. When a child has low regularity, the routine may not match his own biological rhythm, but his healthy development depends on its consistency and stability. Routines and schedules build inner regulation that eventually builds emotional regulation.

Since infancy, Isabel has never had a regular schedule in eating or sleeping patterns. She is three and a half now and still eats and sleeps irregularly and shows no interest in potty training. Mom enrolled her in a new preschool in her neighborhood that is three days a week, hoping that it might help her to have a set routine. She is still in diapers. Her teachers asked Mom and Dad if they would work on potty training at home. They told the teachers they tried for a while but it only frustrated everyone. For now, they all agreed to give it more time and see how Isabel responds, with encouragement from her teachers.

## Strategies to Meet the Needs of a Child Who Has Low Regularity

A child who has difficulty regulating her own eating, sleeping, and elimination, as well as her emotions, will benefit from strategies that support consistency in your program:

### *Look at the behavior through the lens of temperament.*

- Remember that a child who has low regularity may be using a challenging behavior to meet his body's needs, not to push your buttons. He can look like he is being resistant when in fact he is trying to tell you through his behavior that he is hungry or tired.

- As with high regularity, remember that this is his biology. He can gain skills at self-regulation with guidance from an adult and lots of practice of those skills. It's important to realize that he is not going to be highly regulated, but he can be *better* regulated.

- Recognize your own temperament trait related to regularity and how it may or may not match with this child. If you are highly regulated, identify where you might have challenges with a child who is irregular. Look for ways to adapt your environment so he will feel more comfortable and have opportunities to expand his ability to wait longer or pause more.

### Look for any pattern from the child that you can build on.

- Support her regularity where it is naturally expressed by her. Build on that natural tendency, whether it is the same way she likes to start her day or regularly eating at one snacktime over another time. Seeing any patterns may take a while.

- Record her behaviors for a couple of weeks. Does she get crabby at certain times of the day? Are the difficult times consistent? What is happening right before and right after the behavior? Is this a trigger for hunger or sleepiness?

- Once you can identify a pattern to her behaviors, build on that. Make sure she gets a snack at the time of day when you have identified a consistent challenging behavior. Support her each day with the snack until you form a routine. Creating external routines for her will build internal regulation.

### Continue to promote routines that help a child build internal regulation.

- Have a consistent schedule so the child is used to the same thing every day. This builds biological regulation as she follows the schedule and gets used to doing the same thing at the same time every day.

- Consider making him an individual picture schedule to follow that consists of small squares fastened together to represent each transition. Let him keep it in his cubby to refer to throughout the day.

- Tie the same event to each day of the week to reinforce a schedule. For example, every Friday is ask-and-tell day, every Tuesday is pajama pant day, and so on. This is an effective way to build another routine for the child that supports his regulatory system.

- Build on any regularity the child may express. For instance, if he always wants to play with building bricks first thing in the morning, make that a consistent part of the schedule for him.

***Help a child learn her body signals for different rhythms like eating, fatigue, excitement, elimination, and so on.***

- Talk to her about what it feels like when she is hungry. What does her tummy feel like? What does her mouth feel like? When she is tired, how does she feel?

- Remind her during the day about these signs. "Do you think you are hungry now? How does it feel?"

- Talk about thinking ahead of the feeling, if she is old enough. "How do you know when you are going to get hungry?" This can help establish a pattern for the child of reading cues for hunger and possibly setting some routine for eating with regularity.

***Encourage parents to use consistent child care routines.***

- As much as possible, ask parents to use the same drop-off and pickup times to build a consistent routine for their child. Explain why this will help their child.

- Another routine could be packing the backpack with the child every night before bedtime as a nighttime ritual. Doing it in the same way at the same time is the important part for them to practice.

- If the child struggles with eating breakfast some mornings, have parents bring the same snack to child care.

- Consider having "child care shoes" or something that is tied to only the child care setting.

***Promote emotional regulation.***

- Use books that teach feelings and words for feelings. Read them in groups with all children and one-on-one with this child to encourage emotional literacy.

- Practice feelings words with the child by asking, "How do you feel when you are angry? How fast does your heart beat? Can we help it slow down?" Offer encouragement when he expresses an emotion.

- Build emotional-literacy skills so the child has expressive and receptive language tools to regulate his feelings and build impulse control. All this contributes to greater overall regulation.

- For example, let the children in your program use mirrors to make expressions of the feelings you are reading in a book so they see what happy looks like on their faces. Have them turn to a neighbor and make a happy face. Have them draw pictures of themselves when they feel that way. Share the pictures in circle time.

- Put up a feelings chart with a mirror or reflective surface nearby so the child can look at the feelings on the chart and make those expressions in the mirror to see what his feelings look like.

## Story of Success

As an infant, Malcolm had very irregular patterns of sleeping and eating. He might feed every hour one night and then sleep four to six hours the next night. It was hard for his parents to figure out any kind of schedule for when he would be hungry or sleepy. When he went to child care at six months old, his first provider told them after two weeks that he cried too much and upset the other children, so she couldn't take care of him anymore. Fortunately, a close friend told them of a family child care provider in their neighborhood who had an infant opening. Malcolm has been in this home child care for three months and is doing better with his schedule. While he still has irregular patterns of eating, he is tending to sleep with more regularity. His child care provider says he is a precious baby and she can't imagine not having him there!

# 10

# Sensory Awareness—Too Hot, Too Cold, or Just Right

"It's too noisy in here"; "The food is too spicy"; "My socks make my feet too hot." Children have their own sensory threshold early on. We want to help them find, like Goldilocks, what's just right so they can put their energy into play and learning, not seeking or avoiding sensations around them.

As a temperament trait, sensory awareness is a child's level of awareness of his surroundings through his seven senses. His sensory awareness, whether high or low or in between, will determine how he responds to the sensory input he is receiving through the following senses:

- **Visual Sense:** Information is gathered through our eyes using the visual sense. A child can be overstimulated by all the color, pictures, or clutter in a room and need to retreat from it, sometimes using a behavior that will get him removed from the room. Or he may seek more sensory input by looking for electronics that have pictures and light-up features or by wanting to paint with the brightest colors.

- **Auditory Sense:** Our ears are the mechanism for gathering input for the auditory sense. Child care can sometimes be a noisy place. A child may be able to tolerate only a certain noise level before he puts his hands over his ears and says, "Stop." Other children will seek out the loudest toys or games and not be bothered at all. They may even yell, "Louder, Teacher!"

- **Gustatory Sense:** This is the sense of taste that is provided through what we put in our mouths. A child's sensitivity awareness will often be seen in taste if he won't eat certain textures or flavors of food. On the other hand, a child may eat anything you serve him because he has very low sensitivity and it all tastes good to him.

- **Olfactory Sense:** The olfactory sense is the sense of smell that comes through our noses. A child can be highly reactive to strong smells like spices or soaps or may hardly notice the smell of what is being served for lunch.

- **Tactile Sense:** The sense of touch comes through our largest organ, the skin. Our nerves tell us if we are touching something, and our brain processes if we like the feel of that touch or not. A child may seek a favorite touch, like his blankie with the satin edging, and use that for soothing. Another child may be very averse to rough textures or the seam in his socks.

- **Vestibular Sense:** A child's sense of balance comes through his inner ear and is called the vestibular sense. It tells a child where his body is in relation to the world around him. He may not know why he feels off balance at times but may seek ways to meet this need by swinging or rocking vigorously. Or, conversely, he may avoid any type of input that comes from being off balance and so won't climb the slide or stairs without holding someone's hand.

- **Proprioceptive Sense:** The sense of input into muscles and joints is the proprioceptive sense. It involves the muscles, joints, and ligaments that help a child's coordination and movement. Some children will seek this sensory input and need lots of physical play while other children will avoid it by not playing rough-and-tumble or using gross-motor skills.

Sensory awareness can be at the root of many challenging behaviors in the child care setting. A child may be overly sensitive to a sensation that doesn't even register for others, like a smell no one else notices or a tag on the back of his shirt. By contrast, a child may be undersensitive to sensory stimulation; this child may not seem affected by loud booms or scratchy clothes or may be able to spin forever on a merry-go-round. It is important to note here that sensory awareness as a temperament trait is a natural part of how the child reacts to stimulation in the environment based on his own sensory system. It is not a disorder or a dysregulation that can be part of a disability like sensory processing disorder. Sensory processing disorder occurs when the brain has trouble receiving and responding to the information taken in through a child's senses. Taste, smell, movement, or other sensory data can be misread by the brain and signal a different response than would be typical for someone without the disorder. For the purposes of this chapter, we are talking only about high and low sensory awareness as a temperament trait and not a disorder.

As a temperament trait, sensory awareness also refers to emotional sensitivity as well as to the physical sensitivity from the input to his seven senses. A child may seem hypersensitive in regard to her expression of emotions and reactions to others. She may cry more easily than others, for example. On the other hand, a child may seem to have more of a flat affect or lack of reaction to the emotions of peers. In this case, her emotional sensitivity would be low. Emotional sensitivity is sometimes regarded as the tenth temperament trait, though here we will wrap emotional and physical sensitivity together.

A child is seen as flexible if she has low sensitivity needs and is also regular and adaptable, with a positive mood and low intensity. A child with high sensory awareness is in the feisty temperament type if she is also highly active, intense, negative in mood, and low in regularity. In looking at both high and low sensory awareness, challenges come to the early educator when a child is in a situation where the sensory environment isn't matching his sensory need. Being aware as a teacher of a dominant trait like sensory under- or overstimulation helps us make adjustments so a child can feel like he belongs in just the right place.

> Adahy is two and a half. He refuses to eat any food that has a sauce or flavoring added to it, including cheese. He will eat the cheese by itself but not mixed in. Even when his provider adds a bit of salt to plain macaroni, he says it is way too salty and he can't eat it. She mostly accommodates his wishes, but she sometimes puts a teaspoon of a slightly flavored food on his plate for him to try if he wants to.

## How Does a Child Express High Sensory Awareness?

High sensory awareness means a child is more tuned in to the environment, whether it is the physical or the emotional setting. Physically, a child with high sensory awareness may be sensitive to the noise level of the program, the smells coming from the kitchen, the lighting, and other sensory input from the environment. Emotionally, a child who is high in sensory awareness may be responsive to moods of other children or staff, especially if a child is having a tantrum or crying. Emotional sensitivity is subtler than sensitivity that comes through the sensory system; it may have less of an impact on behaviors than overawareness of tactile stimulation, for example. Tactile overstimulation could be pervasive for a child if he is bothered by a texture he is wearing that he cannot remove.

### Challenging Behaviors

High sensory awareness can also be challenging for a child in child care because of the wide range of sounds, smells, and other visual experiences that are part of a lively child care group. If a young child has difficulty regulating himself, he can easily become overwhelmed by the environment.

A child with high sensitivity might use a challenging behavior, like biting or hitting, to get himself removed from a busy or overstimulating room. If he gets sent to the director's office where it is quiet, he has figured out a strategy to meet his sensory needs. We want to teach him more adaptive and appropriate tools.

A child with high sensory awareness may object to wearing certain textiles or complain about tags in her clothes to the point of refusing to wear them. This can mean the child arrives at child care in the morning already highly aroused after a power struggle with Mom or Dad. She may have a hard time calming back down, and her agitation may result in a fight right off the bat with a friend who doesn't want to give her a turn.

A child who has high sensitivity may say that food that tastes normal to adults or peers is too spicy or too salty. He may refuse to eat a certain colored food, like anything green. Feeding everyone in the program and still adapting to one or more who won't eat what you have prepared is challenging. It can make the teacher frustrated and result in power struggles. (See chapter 8 for strategies to avoid power struggles.)

A child with high sensitivity in one or more areas may become overwhelmed with the sensory input that is part of the normal child care environment. This can cause a *distress tantrum*, a tantrum that occurs when his body simply cannot take any more stimuli. He reacts by melting down and shutting down the input. Usually a child who is having a distress tantrum will be hard to soothe and simply needs a calm place to organize his sensory system again. This is not a challenging behavior that the child is using to get his way but rather a biological reaction to overstimulation.

High sensitivity in emotional expression can be challenging if a child cries easily over small slights, but it can also add a lot of excitement to a classroom. A child who laughs easily with great glee can be a delight as well!

> Crimson is four and has been in Ms. Amelie's family child care since she was a toddler. She is very sensitive to what other children say to her or what they do when they play with her. Falling on the floor in tears while playing with a peer and saying loudly, "Everyone is so mean to me!" is not uncommon for her.

## Positive Behaviors

A child who is emotionally sensitive may be more perceptive of another child's feelings, for instance, if she is sad or being left out by others. This can make him a more empathetic peer. The child has a positive influence on the classroom as a whole when he can sense what might be less obvious to the busy teacher or child care provider.

A child who is more sensitive to her own senses tends to be more creative in her expressions, including using art or drama. This can be fun in a classroom where she can lead others in inventive ways to use the dramatic play center or art area. A child who is sensitive to the moods or feelings of others will likely be a calming and soothing presence for her friends when they are upset or have hurt themselves.

A child who has high sensory awareness of her vestibular or proprioceptive system isn't going to take risks like other children who are less aware of their bodies. She will be more cautious and not climb or run where she feels unsafe. She may model safer play on the outside equipment or even caution children who are using the slide or bars recklessly. She can be a good influence for a child whose gross-motor movements are less proficient.

We can sometimes use a helper who lets us know the noise level has gotten too loud and we need to take a pause and calm everyone down. She can be a bell-wether for intensity of noise or smells in our programs.

## Effects on the Child's Relationships with Peers and Adults

Relationships, as we have seen throughout this book, can be hard for children to build and maintain. They need adults to guide them because they are inexperienced and don't know all the ins and outs of socially accepted behavior yet. Temperament traits can make relationships even more difficult while a child is learning how to manage his own feelings and reactions. High sensitivity is a trait that can put barriers in the way of friendships because of the extreme range of reactions the child's sensory system elicits.

A child who doesn't like loud noise may avoid certain activity areas or games. If he is playing with a group and he puts his hands over his ears and says, "Too loud," his friends might think they have done something wrong, or they might think he is too hard to play around. Peers may avoid a child who seems to "overreact" to sensory input, especially if it results in emotional outbursts. Children get worried when another child cries a lot or gets upset around them, especially when they can't see how too much smell or sound is bothering him. He may startle easily at sounds no one else notices, like when the lights make a buzzing sound. His agitation at sensory experiences could cause anxiousness in others close to him.

If a child is spending much of her energy avoiding sensory stimulation, she may not be putting energy into playing with her friends. Her play may be interrupted by what bothers her in the environment, and at some point, peers may think she's not that fun to play with anymore. On the plus side, a child who is highly sensitive may also be very empathetic to her peers. Friends may seek her out because of her kindness and willingness to listen and understand them.

If the child care provider is low on sensory awareness or even in the middle range, understanding a child who is high on sensitivity will be more difficult. If you barely notice the noise level in a room of fifteen preschoolers, a child who is crying because someone is talking too loud will be harder to fathom. If someone says, "It's too spicy," and you know that all you added was a little salt and pepper, you will likely be annoyed until you understand his sensory needs. Teachers who do not realize a child's high sensory awareness might see challenging behaviors as deliberate or as pushing their buttons. For instance, some behaviors that could baffle a teacher include the following:

- an infant crying in reaction to different levels of teachers' voices in the infant room

- a toddler who refuses to eat anything that feels mushy in his mouth

- a preschooler becoming inconsolable when it is time to go outside because his sock is bunched up in his snow boots

## Effects on Play Skills and Other Development

A child with high sensory awareness will be tuned in to all the sights and sounds of the classroom or family child care center. Play may be harder in some areas of the program than others, depending on the child's sensory needs and what kind of match the activity center is to his needs.

For instance, a child who cannot tolerate the sounds of outside play with all of the stomping or yelling could miss the gross-motor play that he needs. If he has proprioceptive sensitivity, he may avoid input to his muscles or joints, which can cause delays in physical development. Getting this child moving may be challenging. Look for ways you can incorporate what he enjoys into more action. For instance, if he likes dramatic play, maybe dress-up can be part of a dance. A gym can be overwhelming for a child with high sensory awareness. Noise and light are amplified. You can help a child to be more successful in group games or sports by making adaptations, such as muffling sounds with earplugs or headphones for some of the time period. Frequent breaks may be helpful.

Play skills that are dependent on interaction with others are hindered if the child isn't engaging consistently with her peers. A child with high emotional sensitivity may be more tearful than a typical child. This can be upsetting to her peers, and young children can be frightened away by a friend whose emotions are intense and easily provoked.

A child who feels overloaded by her sensory system may shut down in the child care setting just because her body feels overwhelmed. Or she might use a behavior that has worked in the past to get her sent to the nurse's office or sent home where she knows she is more comfortable. So much energy is going into avoiding a sensation that she may be missing out on the learning that is going on around her. Your adaptations within the environment can make a significant difference in her ability to cope with the sensory setting.

Malcolm sees his friend Zhou and yells across the room, "Come over here and play with me." He is banging two large blocks together in rhythm as he dances. Zhou puts her hands over her ears and says, "Too loud!"

## Strategies to Meet the Needs of a Child Who Has High Sensory Awareness

High sensory awareness can be hard for a child if she is not in a supportive environment. A child can feel out of control when the room seems overwhelming to her but she isn't sure why. Remember how young and inexperienced children are! The sensory system is complex, and children don't have the language to express what their bodies are saying to them. For children in your programs who have high sensory awareness, strategies to help them be successful can include the following:

***First and foremost, recognize that high sensory awareness is part of a child's natural wiring.***

- The seven senses that comprise the sensory system are complicated. If a child is sensitive to one or more of them, recognize and appreciate how difficult the world can be for him! Because he doesn't have the word for *headache*, he may not understand why a certain room makes him feel like his head is exploding, but the overhead lights are triggering a physical reaction for him.

- You can make adaptations to help the early childhood setting seem less like an assault on a child's senses, like putting diffusers on bright overhead lights or giving him noise-canceling headphones. However, a child with high sensory awareness will always react more strongly to stimulation than other children. Being proactive to sensory input that you think could be troubling can prevent challenging behaviors before they occur.

***Help a child understand her own body.***

- Depending on her age, help her know what her body feels like when it gets too much stimulation. (See chapter 9 for strategies for overregulation.) For example, when it's too noisy for too long, does it make her head hurt? You could ask her, "When your head hurts, what is happening around you?"

- Give one or two tools for dealing with the overstimulation. Practice the tools so she knows how to use them when she needs to. If she has to put on noise-canceling headphones, she needs to know where they are kept. What are the rules for using headphones? How long can she keep them on? You and she can talk about the best way to help her be part of the program and still get sensory breaks.

- Teach her to take a break, such as going to the reading nook or a quiet space. Help her plan ahead where her take-a-break space is.

- Teach her how to ask for help. If the room is too noisy or she feels dizzy on the playground, give her words to tell the teacher. Take it seriously when she tells you, and try to change the environment for her.

### Give him some control over the environment.

- To gain some regulation on overstimulation, a child needs to gradually increase his tolerance. Give him opportunities to control the environmental factors that bother him, being mindful of when it is too much. For example, if he is very sensitive to sound, ask him to help you determine on a scale of one to five how loud the room is. If five is too loud, ask him how to make it a four or a three. Depending on what he says, ask him for some ideas to bring down the volume. Try one or two of his ideas for a few minutes. Help him see that sometimes a two is possible, like if everyone can whisper for a little while, but that he is also okay when the noise level is at a three. Celebrate his successes when he manages louder noise for longer periods of time without complaints.

- If he has olfactory sensitivity, let him help you choose what seasoning to put on the food for lunch sometimes, if possible. With his help, try to gradually increase the seasoning on his plate. Replace something you might be using with the other children that is stronger in flavor with a substitute that still has a flavor he can taste.

### Recognize the child's triggers for overstimulation.

- Adults may need to help a child recognize her triggers for overstimulation until she has better self-regulation skills.

- Give verbal feedback on a child's arousal level, like "Your engine seems really fast; can we slow it down?" Help the child understand what this means. (See chapter 8 for more strategies on overstimulation.)

- Know the child's limits for certain types of stimulation. Be prepared to step in with a strategy to help a child stay on an even keel. For instance, if you know a fire drill is going to take place, ensure that the child with sensory issues for sound has earplugs or sound-muffling headphones.

*As with all temperament traits, avoid labeling a child.*

- Be careful not to call the child "picky," "high maintenance," or "spoiled." Names hurt children's self-esteem. Other children hear us use them and will repeat them to the child.

- Rather than label a child's natural wiring, see it as his strength. His high sensitivity to the world around him doesn't mean he is out of touch with reality; it means he is tuned in to things we might not see, like the sound of a bird in the courtyard or the feelings of a peer who was left out.

*Create a sensory-free zone.*

- Provide a space that has few distractions where a child can go for a break from sensory experiences. If you have a take-a-break space, keep it free from pictures and color. Limit what goes into that space, such as toys. Keep lighting as dim as possible.

- Practice what the space is for. Explain to children that they can go there to calm down and relax. Talk about how their bodies feel when they are excited and when they are calm.

*Offer a comfortable learning space in your environment with few distractions.*

- Avoid the use of bright fluorescent lights where possible. Use floor lamps to help a child who becomes overstimulated visually. Consider diffusers on the overhead lights to soften lighting.

- Paint walls in a soft color. Bright primary colors are alerting and visually stimulating rather than calming.

- As much as possible, keep clutter out of sight. Cover open cabinets with curtains. Take most posters and pictures off the walls. To avoid visual overstimulation, consider not hanging anything from the ceiling.

- Arrange quiet activities like art and reading near each other and away from noisier activity areas.

*Consider the intensity of the sensory experience you are offering in your activities and materials.*

- Think about how you can change the intensity by using alternative materials; for example, let a child with sensory sensitivity finger paint with gloves on. Or consider whether the lighting in some rooms can be turned down for some activities. Could the glue be changed to a scent-free version?

- Can some of the noisier toys be offered for outside play? Do you tend to play music during the day? If so, think about music-free zones or classical music.

### *Give a child words to express how she is feeling.*

- A child may not understand what her body is telling her, so help her practice words for feelings. You might give her phrases to use like "My ears can't listen anymore" or "My eyes are seeing too much."

- To help teach words, use books on feelings. After reading a book on emotions, use group time to ask everyone, "How does your body feel when you are angry/happy/sad?" Let them talk about what they can do with their feelings, like talk to a teacher or take a break.

- Hold up mirrors so children can practice seeing the feelings on their own faces.

- Posters of children showing various feelings help a child see a feeling on another's face and relate it to her own. This develops empathy and also an awareness for all feelings.

- Normalize feelings by expressing them yourself, like saying, "I was sad last night because my puppy was sick." Children see that you have big feelings, too, but you are still there to take care of them.

Giving children words for their feelings is important for high and low emotional sensitivity. Helping a child learn to express a "big" feeling like frustration or anger can prevent a challenging behavior from occurring if the child has time to process her emotions and tell the teacher or a peer how she is feeling.

### Story of Success

David is in Mr. Han's preschool classroom with six other boys and three girls. David likes all the children and usually likes to go to most activity centers—except large-muscle play, which is in a big, open room. It has high ceilings and very bright lights, and when all the kids are playing with balls and other gross-motor games, it is very loud. David is very sensitive to noise, and sometimes he puts his hands over his ears to try to stop the screaming sounds. Lately he has been running into other boys and knocking them down because then he has to leave play and go to the director's office for a while. Mr. Han has noticed a pattern of aggression when David seems to get overwhelmed by the noise, and believes

David uses this behavior to be removed from the loud sensory experience. He talked to David about using sound-muffling headphones when the sound gets to be too much. David can wear them and still hear the ball noise and the kids talking to him, but it is a softer sound. So far David has worn them for a week and hasn't had any incidents with hitting or knocking over his peers.

## How Does a Child Express Low Sensory Awareness?

Low sensory awareness means a child will not have as much reaction to the environment—for instance, smells, sounds, or temperature—as her peers and may not notice the sensory input that bothers a child with higher awareness. It takes more stimulation of her senses for this child to have a response; for instance, she would notice a fire alarm but not the buzzing of a fluorescent light. A child with low sensory awareness will be in the flexible temperament type if other traits like regularity, adaptability, and low intensity are also part of her disposition. She simply isn't as reactive as other children to what is happening to her senses.

### Challenging Behaviors

While this child may tend to be more flexible in nature, sometimes his lack of sensory awareness will present challenges to his providers and friends in child care. A child with low sensory awareness may be *sensory seeking*, which means he will look for ways to get sensory stimulation. For instance, he may need proprioceptive input and may intuitively try to bring stimulation to his muscles and joints by stomping his feet or marching loudly. The need for sensory stimulation may be the reason some children run into peers and give big bear hugs. They may gravitate to louder, noisier toys in seeking auditory or visual stimulation.

A child with low emotional sensitivity may not be as sensitive to a peer's emotions and might hurt feelings and not seem empathetic. This could result in a peer becoming upset and withdrawing from him.

A child with low sensory awareness may be more prone to accidents because she may be more of a risk-taker than her peers. Because her threshold for sensory input is greater, she may handle physical hurts differently than a typical child. She could put other children at risk, too, if she isn't afraid to climb high or jump from a slide.

She may not be reactive to things that might bother another child, like getting gravel in her shoes on the playground or being thirsty after a hard play. She isn't going to complain about the temperature in the room or say it is too hot to go outside.

## Positive Behaviors

You will see behaviors that are typical of a child who mostly goes with the flow. He may be easygoing and flexible because he is not hindered by sensory overstimulation that can inhibit other children. This makes for easier transitions because he isn't trying to compensate for sensory input as he moves from center to center, like adjusting to the lighting or the sound variations from space to space.

It is easier to introduce new activities, play materials, and foods to a child who isn't bothered by textures or smells. He may sleep through any noises or interruptions at naptime.

He may not be as sensitive to other children's teasing or slights because he isn't as emotionally tuned in or sensitive to others, which can keep him from striking back at a peer or being upset. This can also cause some challenging behaviors if he ignores the feelings of others because he is unaware that he has hurt someone's feelings.

A child who has low sensitivity will be more flexible, making it easier to adapt the environment to his needs. His sensory system will not cause overreactions to the child care setting, giving him more opportunities to learn and develop.

> Phoenix is playing next to Amaia in the sandbox outside when a fire engine roars by with loud sirens. Amaia says, "That is too loud; it scares me," and Phoenix replies, "I like fire engines because they are my favorite color, red."

## Effects on the Child's Relationships with Peers and Adults

The effect of low sensory awareness as a temperament trait on a child's relationships with peers and adults will likely be minimal. As with other traits that do not cause typical challenging behaviors like aggression or emotional outbursts, a child with low sensitivity will usually not react to her environment with great highs and lows. This can make her more resilient than a typical peer, resulting in fewer of the emotional pitfalls that can get in the way of friendships, especially as children get older. A provider should be aware of how a child's low sensitivity to her sensory system or her emotions could impact her relationships with friends.

A child with low emotional sensitivity may not pick up on the social cues of peers, like if his playmate is sad. It could mean he doesn't react to this friend's sadness in a caring way that builds goodwill and friendship but instead ignores the emotion or, worse, says something like "Why are you being a baby?" We would expect this to be more of an issue with a preschooler than a toddler, who isn't going to be as tuned in to feelings yet.

He may react inappropriately at times to another child's distress if he himself does not understand a physical reaction the peer is having because his sensory system doesn't register the same way. For instance, a child might become startled and scared by the noise of a fire engine going by. The child who underreacts might not notice this as a big event and not understand the fearfulness, maybe making his friend feel silly for being upset. On the other hand, a child who doesn't overreact to environmental changes or fluctuations will be an easy companion. He probably won't get upset at much and will be a friend whose moods are dependable.

For adults, the relationship with a child who has low sensitivity will be easier to maintain than other temperament traits. She isn't bothered when there is something new going on and doesn't notice tacos cooking or the windows being open. As mentioned above, the main concern will be in keeping her safe from risky behaviors if she tends to be sensory seeking, like climbing or running where it isn't safe. If she has low regularity and high adaptability, she will join new activities quickly and try new things first, whether it's a change in the sensory table or a different kind of vegetable.

## Effects on Play Skills and Other Development

Play for a child with low sensory awareness means a lot of exploration and adventures since he will rarely worry about how the environment is affecting his sensory system. In fact, he will look for sensory experiences that increase his opportunities to learn and develop. As an example, he might try new movements in games like Simon Says because his vestibular sense doesn't tell him he's off balance. He may even seek input by wanting to stand on his head or lean to the side. Or he will try out all the costumes in dramatic play, using his imagination and adding to his vocabulary as he interacts with peers. Additionally, he won't notice when the sand gets in his shoes, so he will keep using the climber outside, increasing his muscle strength and coordination skills. He will probably eat anything that is offered at snack or lunch, because a child with low sensory awareness is rarely a picky eater. Good nutrition supports overall development and keeps children healthier.

Low emotional sensitivity may interfere with a child's development in terms of friendship competencies, though. We want children, beginning with toddlers and continuing through the preschool years, to develop social-emotional skills like sharing, cooperating, problem-solving, and empathizing with peers. If a child has low emotional sensitivity, in sensing either her own feelings or the feelings of others, she may miss chances to make meaningful relationships with peers and grow her social-emotional skills.

For example, a young girl may be playing with a friend who gets hurt or upset in the course of their interaction. Because of low emotional sensory awareness on her part, she may not soothe him or seek help for him. She may not ask for help for herself, either, when she doesn't get asked to join friends in a game. She may not realize when she is being left out or even bullied by others. If she does think something is wrong with the way a friend is treating her, she may brush it off because she doesn't tend to make a big deal out of her feelings.

Jansen has come back into the three-year-old classroom with Kaleo after playing outside together. Kaleo turns to him and says that Jansen wasn't supposed to be the line leader today because it was Kaleo's turn. Kaleo says that makes him really mad. Jansen looks blankly at Kaleo and goes over to the snack table without him. Jansen tends to have trouble sensing the emotions of others, and in this case, he doesn't even realize his friend is upset with him.

## Strategies to Meet the Needs of a Child Who Has Low Sensory Awareness

A child in our early childhood programs with low sensory awareness needs to be supported, too, but may not ask for help in as obvious a way as a child who is overly sensitive to the environment or his emotions. He can tend to be overlooked because he doesn't tell us that he feels unhappy or hasn't been included in some activity. For a child who has low sensory awareness, the following strategies can help engage him in the environment while increasing his sensory experiences:

### *Provide a rich sensory experience.*

- Use a sensory table. Change the materials often so a child can have varied interactive experiences. For instance, if you have sand in the table, add scoops and sieves. Bring in play materials from other areas that extend the tactile experience. The goal is to give a child great sensory experiences to increase his awareness of his senses.

- Change the textures offered in the sand table—experiment with bird seed, different types of clay, colored sand, shells, and outdoor items like pinecones and leaves. This will give a child low on sensory awareness an opportunity to try new textures and sensations.

- Have books in your reading nook and story time that have textures on the pages for children to touch and talk about with each other. Help them learn to describe how different materials feel, like rough or soft, and connect the sensations to emotions. "Does this feel good to your touch, or do you prefer something different?"

- Include a wide variety of play clothes in the dramatic play area, like silk, fur, leather, plastic, hats, and masks. If the child with low sensory awareness has a favorite dramatic play activity, like firefighter, add more variety to the firefighter options to increase the sensory experience.

### Incorporate many opportunities for movement throughout the day.

- Have children march or move in creative ways, like dancing when transitioning from one activity to another, to encourage proprioceptive input to muscles and joints.

- Think of how you can let children move in different ways before and after a quiet activity to wake up their muscles and joints. For instance, try skating on paper plates or having an indoor "freeze" game.

- Give a child with low sensory awareness the job of trying to "hold up" or "push down" the walls while waiting in line. This gives sensory input into shoulders and arms to wake up the proprioceptive sense.

- Use stretchy bands, scarves, or streamers to help children move in large-group exercise and play.

### Create a sensory box.

- Make a box that is filled with lots of textures, textiles, and items with unusual shapes and sizes. You could use the box in circle time or one-on-one with a child who is low on sensory awareness. A child can guess what the objects are or talk about how something feels, what it reminds her of, or where she thinks it came from.

- Expand the sensory box to include other sensory experiences. For example, take a shell from the box and use it to create an art project using finger paints or other media the child can touch and feel.

### Create a fidget basket with sensory options.

- A fidget basket can be filled with play choices, including squishy balls, play-dough, glitter wands, and other small sensory items. Some materials will be more appealing to a child with low awareness than others, so try to make it as varied as possible.

- Let a child have access to the fidget basket throughout the day to increase sensory input and also increase alertness and engagement through tactile stimulation. A sensory basket can be used during transitions to keep children engaged and also during circle time to increase attention.

***Help a child become more aware of input to his sensory system by pointing it out to him.***

- Talk about the smells you notice or noises you are hearing to increase his awareness of the sensations. If you can hear a siren in the distance, talk about what makes that noise. What does it sound like? Is it loud or soft? How does it make your ears feel? What happens when you cover your ears?

- Encourage a child to touch materials as you are talking to him, increasing his sensory experience and awareness. For example, outside you can talk about the blue sky and have him hold his hand up to touch the air. What does air feel like? Is the grass soft or hard? What does a leaf feel like?

***Intentionally introduce new sensory experiences through your daily activities.***

- Talk about the food you are serving for snack or lunch. Is it crunchy or soft? What does it smell like? What color is it? Ask the child with low sensory awareness if the taste reminds her of anything or makes her feel a certain way.

- Talk about the texture of the things around you; for instance, is her shirt soft? What else is soft? Is the rug on the floor soft too? Or is it scratchy?

***For emotional undersensitivity, teach a child words for his feelings.***

- Give a child words for his peers' feelings, like "Susan is mad because you took her baby doll" and "How can you help Susan feel better now?" If he can't express how he thinks she feels, give him prompts like "Do you think she is sad?" and then talk about why his action made her sad. Ask, "How can we change her feelings?"

- Use books that illustrate children displaying different behaviors, for instance, how Sophie solves her anger in Molly Bang's *When Sophie Gets Angry—Really, Really Angry*. Take opportunities to discuss the book by asking, "What do you do when you get really angry?" or "What did Sophie do? Is that something you would do also?" Encourage children to draw pictures about the books you read, giving them an outlet for drawing their feelings.

- Point out when a child expresses his feelings to others or recognizes feelings in a peer. Encourage him by telling him what a good friend he was. Offer positive reinforcement when he responds to a peer.

***Check in with this child.***

- Stay tuned in to her sensory needs, knowing that this child may be unaware of the lack of input she is receiving through sensory experiences. If she avoids or is seeking input, take note and ensure that she can get what she needs without using a challenging behavior.

- Look for disengagement or a lack of participation in a particular area of play that uses a key sense. For instance, if she never plays in gross-motor activities, she is missing proprioceptive input. She may not seek it out because it isn't a need for her. Look for ways to increase this sensory experience for her.

- Be aware that all children are on a developmental continuum when it comes to social-emotional development. Emotional sensitivity will impact a child's emotional development, but so will your physical and emotional environment, your interactions, and peer play opportunities.

## Story of Success

Elizabeth likes to be in the middle of the action in her family child care program, even though she is one of the younger preschoolers. She likes to try to keep up with the older children. Sometimes she doesn't stop to think before she does something, and she has gotten hurt at times. Her provider is helping her think more before she moves too fast into play with older children. So sometimes her provider says, "Is that a one, a two, or a three?" when Elizabeth is going to try something new. A three means it takes a lot of her arms and legs to do it. She can still try it, but she is learning to think it through first.

# 11

## Mood—Sunny or Cloudy Day

Some infants naturally smile early and at everyone they see, while others need to be coaxed and coaxed to get the slightest glimmer of a smile.

As a temperament trait, the quality of a child's mood is measured on a continuum from negative or pessimistic on one side to positive or optimistic on the other. Most children will fall in the middle or toward the optimistic side of the sorter. Mood is one indicator of the temperament types when other temperament traits are dominant:

**Flexible:** positive mood, high or average regularity, high adaptability, low intensity, and low sensory awareness

**Feisty:** pessimistic mood, high activity, high intensity, high distractibility, high sensory awareness, low regularity

Since temperament is the natural wiring of a child, mood is simply the lens through which she inherently views the world. Some children are perpetually happy from early on, while other babies begin life fussier and harder to soothe. A child who is more serious than typical-aged peers may have a countenance that seems more like a frown or a stern face than a child who is more easygoing.

A child on the positive end of the temperament trait may always seem to be upbeat and not have the usual ups and downs more typical for her age group. A child on the negative end of mood may see the adverse aspects of a situation first, like how hot it is outside when going out to play. It may be hard to get this child to see the good in the situation without a lot of encouragement from the provider.

A child on the positive side tends to be more optimistic about circumstances, like how lucky he is to get to play outside on the swings again. He seems cheerful if it's rainy and outside play is moved indoors or if it is sunny and that means they get to go out.

Mood, as a temperament trait, is determined by the genetics of a child. If Mom or Dad or a grandparent tended toward a particular mood disposition, then we would say the child inherited it from that family member. But mood as a temperament trait is also influenced by the environment and, as seen in types listed above, other temperament traits the child may have. Consequently, if a child tends to be more on the gloomy side, she will be happier when she gets to choose activities that she really likes, and that will affect her overall mood. Goodness of fit, as explained in chapter 2, informs the provider on what kinds of activities will best build on the child's innate disposition toward seriousness/negativity or positivity. You can ask yourself these questions:

- How do we encourage a child to use a sunnier lens without trying to push our attitudes on him?

- In what ways do we point out the brighter side of a situation to ease a child into a less somber mood?

- How do we support a generally happy child when he is having a bad day?

If we know that a child's overall disposition is feisty instead of flexible, we can follow strategies in previous chapters for adapting the environment, our activities, and our relationship with the child to help her reach positive developmental outcomes, regardless of natural temperament differences.

Wee all have heard comments about someone who sees things through rose-tinted glasses or sees the glass as half empty. When we consider children and the kinds of dispositions they bring to the child care setting, we know that everyone contributes to the diversity of the early childhood community. As with all temperament traits, the world needs different types of personalities to balance it out. A child who is more serious is going to help us pause and consider whether something is really a good idea for all the children. A child who is bubbly and carefree gives us a sense of joy that fuels our passion for our work.

> Conrad bounds into the classroom with gusto. He runs over to his teacher and says, "I'm not staying all day today! I have to go to the dentist, and my dad said he is picking me up before nap! He said the dentist makes your teeth happy."

## How Does a Child Express Negative Mood?

A child closer to the negative end of mood in a temperament sorter is going to be a test more often than a joy to most teachers, given the behaviors that often manifest with negative mood. But if a child has a pessimistic view on the world and also has high adaptability and persistence, that combination might be one that adds a lot of staying power to projects, making her a child you enjoy working with. It has as much to do with the emotional environment of a setting (how accepted does she feel?) as the physical environment (does she have a lot of activities that include her preferences?).

## Challenging Behaviors

A child who defaults to thinking about what is wrong before getting to what is going well is harder for most of us to adjust to. If you tend to be stronger on the positive side of mood, you may struggle with the child who doesn't share your optimism, and see him in a less-than-favorable light. A child on the negative end of mood often shows behaviors that challenge teachers. It may be harder to get positive reactions and responses from him, whether in play with peers or in activities. This can dishearten a teacher who brings in a new treat or has an idea for a fun new project.

A child who has a tendency to think that the sky is falling may be harder to comfort when something goes wrong. Consoling her may take longer if she fears something worse is coming. This child might tend to complain more frequently than other children and for reasons that seem minor to adults. This can cause friction in the ongoing relationships between the child and others. A child whose demeanor seems grumpier or who doesn't seem to outwardly enjoy play is harder to involve in playgroups and may be isolated from peers.

## Positive Behaviors

Some of the positive behaviors you can build on with the child whose mood is more negative involve seeing her as more serious and analytical. These attributes are important in a host of professions the child could choose as an adult. In early childhood, she may solve more complicated puzzles and help others when they can't figure out how to get the right piece in the right place. A child on the pessimistic side may also be more thoughtful before taking action. This thoughtfulness can prevent her from taking part in risky behaviors, like following a peer in jumping from the top of the slide. She may sit back and observe more.

While her face may look serious, this doesn't mean she isn't engaged in what is happening around her. She will join in when she is ready, and she adds a more reflective dimension to what is already going on. A child who is on the serious side may attract friends who like a more subdued play partner rather than an energetic, highly active peer.

The labeling of negative mood and positive mood can lead to unfair judgments about a child. The word *negative* connotes a child who might not be as pleasant as the positive child. When we reframe this side of mood as serious and contemplative, we can see more benefits to a child who is thoughtful and observant.

Adults and peers are generally drawn to outgoing and happy children. A child who seems gloomier is less likely to be the one we are attracted to. As with all temperament traits, once we understand that mood is part of how a child is wired, we can find ways to engage and include that child that fit her temperament.

> Abdul is sitting next to Annette at circle time when the teacher shows the whole group a new turtle that is joining the classroom. Annette cannot contain her excitement and claps her hands. Abdul has a glum look on his face. Finally, he says, "It's just going to die like the last one."

## Effects on the Child's Relationships with Peers and Adults

A child who looks first for what's wrong in a situation or with an activity is harder to get along with. His ability to build relationships with peers will have a lot to do with the personalities of other children and how well the setting responds to individual needs.

For example, if a child with a more pessimistic mood is playing with a child who is high on approach, the play will likely go well. If you have planned activities that build on a child's interest areas, then a child who is on the negative side of mood will have activity areas where he wants to play and engage with others because some of his favorite things are there. He may not show you excitement and pleasure while playing, but his involvement in a game or activity shows you he is participating and interested.

A child's negative mood could discourage other peers from seeking him out to play if the peers are not high on flexible temperament traits. If one friend doesn't get excited to play fire engine or tells his friend he thinks her block building isn't very good, then a less adaptable child might feel hurt and withdraw from play.

Working with a child who tends to see the child care activities, the food, and the planned outings through a lens of pessimism can be emotionally draining. Most adults like to hear, "That was really fun," instead of "Do I have to do it?" With adjustments, though, adults can help a child with a negative natural mood enjoy child care more using the strategies at the end of this chapter.

A negative mood can affect your mood if you are not careful to see it as a temperament trait instead of a criticism of you or your program. When a child's mood is different from your own, coregulation is a tool that helps build a more positive response between a caregiver and a child (Greenspan and Glovinsky 2007). Coregulation refers to the back-and-forth of relating, so the child depends on the caregiver's response and the caregiver is also being influenced by the child's response. Most of the time if you coregulate, you are in sync to calm or soothe a child who may be angry or crabby.

Particularly with a child whose mood may be hard to understand or handle, the child-adult relationship can be interrupted or impaired if the adult cannot understand the emotions the child is expressing. Working with the child to talk about the positives in the environment and helping her learn to express herself with a bit more optimism can help you both have a better experience in child care.

## Effects on Play Skills and Other Development

Any temperament trait that can cause a barrier between a child and peers has the potential to influence the ongoing development of her social-emotional skills. In this case, the barrier is a general pessimistic and sometimes complaining demeanor that isn't inviting to peers. A child who is near the negative end of mood who is not playing and interacting with friends is not learning social competencies. She needs to be able to play successfully to make and keep friendships. A child who is pessimistic about a game being fun, or who thinks the last time she played it didn't turn out the way she had hoped, may refuse to participate in it the next time it is offered. Overcoming her natural tendency to say no first may take more effort than other three- or four-year-olds want to give just to play with someone. Playing games together is an important way for all children to learn across all the developmental domains. If a child isn't playing, she is missing out on some of that learning.

She may tend toward more solitary play because that is where she is most comfortable. She doesn't have to think about what might go wrong. A teacher aware of her preference to avoid others can work on prompts to help her join play with others.

A child who sees the world through a negative lens is going to approach your activities and projects with more reluctance than a child who is cheerful and outgoing. If a child's first reaction is to say no or "I don't like that," and the adults don't help her join an activity, she will likely withdraw. We want to see two-year-olds playing next to peers as they watch each other respond and interact. We want three- and four-year-olds in the dramatic play area, making up characters as they expand their vocabulary, emotional language, and social skills. Any child—whether influenced by negative mood, low approachability, or high sensitivity—who isn't participating in our teaching through play and activities is not developing to her potential.

## Strategies to Meet the Needs of a Child Who Has Negative Mood

A child whose personality is closer to the negative or pessimistic side of mood may bring challenges to his teachers and his ability to make friends. While we do not want to squelch his natural tendency to wait and see as he anticipates an unfavorable outcome, we can help him look for more of the positives around him. Strategies for working with challenging behaviors of the child include the following:

***Help reframe negativity for the child.***

- If a child comes to the program unusually grumpy, look for the reason behind the emotion. Talk about what happened today or last night. Give her a context for then and for now so she can enjoy her experiences in the present rather than dwelling on something that happened at a different time.

- You may use an emotional-literacy tool like a book on feelings and read it together to explore a range of feelings that she may not be expressing. Once you choose a "new" feeling, talk about how that could be spoken or demonstrated by the child. You could also use a feelings poster to help the child recognize her mad or sad self as well as her happy self.

- Build on the positives in a child's affect or behaviors. Express and encourage the child when she is giving positive feedback to others. Provide opportunities for interactions that promote positive feelings, such as with a favorite book or music.

- It takes time to understand the function of a child's behaviors in child care, especially as they relate to emotions. Have patience! Once you understand the reason behind a behavior, you can work to replace the child's challenging behavior with something more appropriate.

***Validate all feelings.***

- Ensure that a child knows that he gets to feel his own feelings. At morning group time, give all children time to talk about how they are feeling, using a feelings cube or feelings wheel, if needed, to encourage emotional literacy. Be careful not to choose favorites when it comes to emotions, especially by praising the child who is cheerful all the time.

- Let every feeling be okay. Don't rush in with "Let's put some sunshine in your cloudy day." Recognize that a child's feelings are worthy. A child, whether he leans toward negative or positive mood, is capable of all the emotions any other child has, so encourage him when he expresses a range of emotions.

### Don't take a negative mood personally.

- Remember that mood is a disposition that is wired from birth. Set aside your perceptions of happy versus pessimistic and revel in the strengths this child brings to your program. If you are struggling to find her strengths, spend a day using observation and recording tools to capture her positive behaviors and interactions.

- Name her seriousness and let her know it is okay to be serious. Talk about how being an observer and thinker is a positive trait. Show her ways this helps you out when she solves a problem or waits before rushing into something.

- Encourage her when she finds solutions to challenges. This is a strength to cultivate. Give her specific praise when she solves a problem.

### Teach socially acceptable ways to express emotions to others.

- A child low on mood may respond to peers or teachers with a headshake or a frown when asked to play a game or participate in an activity. Teach him words for making responses that acknowledge others with respectfulness, even if he doesn't want to play. Using "No, thank you" is an easy reply to practice.

- His comments to friends can be critical instead of supportive. Help him practice phrases that you expect all children to use to show kindness to others. If his peer is showing him an art project, help him have the words to say, "You worked hard" or "You did a nice job."

### Build on what the child likes in order to support her involvement.

- If there is a particular activity that a child really enjoys doing, think about ways you can integrate that activity or parts of it into the daily routine. The child's mood will lift when she knows she gets to do activities she likes.

- Get to know the interests of a child who is more pessimistic and may not readily reveal what she enjoys. Once you know something that engages her and keeps her interest, build on that. For instance, if she complains at cleanup time and doesn't want to do it, but you know she loves all things trains, tell her, "We are loading the train up with toys to go over to the toy bins." Bring her along by joining her likes to tasks or activities that might otherwise cause negative reactions.

## *Avoid labeling.*

- Even as you help the child reframe what it means to be more serious, reframe how you see a child and negative mood. It's easy to say, "He's my grouchy Gus" or "Oscar the Grouch" when referring to him. Use words that build on the strengths of his nature, like how hard he works or how he always finishes jobs.

- Make sure other staff do not use labels for the child instead of using his name, for instance, calling him an Eeyore. Remember that other children often repeat what they hear the adults saying. This can be internalized by the child as a belief that there is something wrong with him.

## *Build on problem-solving skills.*

- A child who is on the pessimistic side of mood may also be analytical because she observes before acting. This means she can often solve a challenging problem more quickly than another child who isn't examining it from all sides. Bring her into problem-solving situations that affirm this natural ability of hers.

- Support this strength by ensuring that she has challenging play activities that meet her developmental level. Provide puzzles that are a little harder than the last ones she completed. The goal is to challenge but not frustrate.

A child on the far side of negative mood brings more pensiveness and sometimes thoughtfulness to our early childhood programs. This quality of being more pessimistic about people or circumstances means this child thinks first before rushing in. She can serve as a bellwether to adults about the meaningfulness of a project or a center you have set up. While adults might need to curb their tendency to want to make a child more joyful and friendly, once you understand the true nature of this child, you will see attributes from her personality that are a benefit to your program.

## Story of Success

When Alexa comes into her classroom at City Nature Center in the mornings, she is usually frowning. When she gets up late, she sometimes doesn't have time for her favorite breakfast at home, waffles. Since Alexa doesn't like to eat breakfast in the car, Ms. Cookie approaches Alexa slowly when she arrives at school with a basket of fruit options and says, "Where would you like to start today? I have your favorite paints already set up in the art room." Alexa reaches for a banana and heads toward art with a small smile on her face.

# How Does a Child Express Positive Mood?

Positive mood is an easy temperament trait to be around. Clustered with other traits like high adaptability and regularity, a child with positive mood is a flexible, easy child. If positive mood is a dominant trait for a child, she is going to be happy and will go with the flow most of the time.

## Challenging Behaviors

As with any trait that makes a flexible personality type, adults can sometimes forget to check in with the child or be as intentional with active supervision because the child is so self-sufficient. You still want to be aware of behaviors that could cause issues for the child. It's possible that a child high on the positive temperament trait may be less thoughtful and serious in how he approaches situations or play with others. Be aware of areas of impulsivity so you can prevent the child from taking risks that could impair safety. In a similar way, a child who is very friendly to everyone might not see the risk in approaching people she doesn't know. Some skills around developing boundaries may be needed.

It is also easy to assume that this child is always cheerful and doesn't have a care in the world. In reality, all children have stressors as part of normal life and need outlets for anxiety and fears. It's important that a child high on positive mood have words for feelings and opportunities to express her emotions too.

## Positive Behaviors

It is easier to imagine positive behaviors rather than challenging ones in a child who has a strong optimistic and positive outlook. This is a child who sees the glass half full and will look for the positive side when something goes wrong. Usually she will be easier to have in a classroom or group setting because she is easygoing and likes to have fun.

A child on the positive end of this temperament trait can lighten up the mood for everyone with her cheerful nature. She comes through the door in the morning happy to be here and is generally pleasant all day. She doesn't tend to complain. More likely, she sees the best in most situations and can help turn around other children in the room who, for instance, might want to fuss about not getting to go outside on a below-zero temperature day.

She doesn't get upset as easily as children who are less positive. Because she sees the upside to a change in the schedule or a new activity, she isn't going to react with resistance to the changes. She is a go-with-the-flow child. Mood tends to stay consistent throughout the day, so a child on the positive end will typically be content and sunny to the last activity.

It makes sense that a child on the far end of positive mood is easier to include in a child care program than a child who has more of the feistier traits. Teachers find it more comfortable to interact with a child who responds with positivity and optimism.

> Penelope is outside on the playground equipment laughing with a couple of friends. Even at the end of the day, she is full of energy and happiness. She sees her nana coming to pick her up, and she screams, "Nana, Nana, Nana!" with a big smile on her face.

### Effects on the Child's Relationships with Peers and Adults

For a child who is outgoing and optimistic, approaching peers to play with her and bringing them into her playgroup is easy. If a child is on the positive end of mood and also high on adaptability and approachability, she may be friends with everyone in the program.

A child who sees the world as a happy place is usually very easy to have around because she isn't going to want to fight with others or complain to the provider. She will probably gladly give up a toy rather than struggle over it, since her optimism tells her she will be able to play with it later. She will tend to engage easily in new projects and bring along other children who might be hesitant or less eager to try something different. Her enthusiasm draws other children to her.

A child with a positive temperament is easily paired with another child who might struggle with making friends. Providing a tool like a buddy bucket for these two children to share can help a less social child learn social competencies. It develops tolerance and empathy in the child who is helping his friend.

However, a child high on optimism can downplay a disappointment a friend is experiencing and not be as sensitive as his friend needs him to be. This kind of obliviousness to others' feelings could interfere with his friendships too.

As a child care provider, your mood is influenced by the moods of the children you care for. Interacting with a child who is positive and cheerful elevates how you are feeling. A child with a positive mood is more even keeled in her interactions with peers throughout the day. She brings an element of positivity that encourages all children.

If you are more on the negative end of mood, you may find the highly positive child a bit unnerving with his constant cheerfulness. While this can be a benefit to the overall climate of the program, you will need to be aware of your temperament differences so you aren't resenting the child's sunniness or becoming impatient with her disposition.

A child who is highly positive and optimistic may not have all the skills to deal with rejection from peers or with interactions that turn aggressive. Your awareness that a child who is generally happy still needs to be able to express disappointment or anger supports his social-emotional growth.

## Effects on Play Skills and Other Development

Play becomes an easy interaction for a child who expects the best to happen, whether in doing an art project or creating new rules for a game. When a child is included by others and even leads the playgroup, the play process greatly enhances her learning. She benefits from the social-emotional development she achieves from being creative, explorative, and involved with others. Even from infancy, a child who smiles more is going to get more attention from adults. We are drawn to a happy baby. A child higher on positive mood gets more affirmation from adults early in life through cooing and "serve and return" and, later, in our general warmth toward the preschooler who is so positive. This attention from adults contributes to a child's having a strong sense of value and self-worth, important to emotional growth and development.

A child who is on the high end of optimism will generally want to please the teacher and her friends. Be aware of a child's tendency to please others and neglect her own needs to be sure she is engaging in activities that enhance her own learning. Also, because she is eager to please, she may be more superficial in interactions with her peers, which could result in less meaningful social relationships for her. Lastly, this inclination to make others happy can mean she engages more in teacher-directed interactions instead of spending time with peers. She could miss out on important social learning in play and conversation with others if she is constantly trying to keep the attention of the teacher. This child will think of ways to overcome obstacles because of her positive outlook. This practice will contribute to her mastery of milestones as she works hard to do it right.

> Miquel and Suni have gone outside to play, holding hands. They are best friends, except for all the other children in class who are also their best friends. Once they get outside, they both run for the slide, laughing because it is their favorite. They wait patiently for two other children to go ahead of them, and then each one goes while the other cheers, "This is SO fun!"

## Strategies to Meet the Needs of a Child Who Has Positive Mood

A child who was born with a disposition of positive mood is going to be pleasant and easy to care for from infancy to preschool. There will be little change in how she sees the world with her hopeful nature as she grows older, especially if the environment supports her positive view.

If a child has a predominantly positive mood, then strategies will revolve around using her positive energy to impact the emotional climate of the program and ensuring that she is learning the skills she needs to be successful too.

### Teach the child sensitivity to the feelings of others.

- Incorporate books about feelings as you talk about what to do when a friend is sad or hurt. Use a feelings chart to help a child see expressions of emotions that he feels or sees in his peers.

- Help a child learn how to express his emotions appropriately to peers and to adults. He may need to practice with you in using expressions or be given some words to start a conversation with a friend. Practice the prompts with him. For instance, help him recognize why exuberance is not an acceptable approach when a friend is sad. While you are not trying to change his natural bend toward being positive, you are giving him tools to grow more empathetic.

### Support the natural tendencies of the highly optimistic child.

- Because she tends to be happy much of the time, ensure that both staff and other children don't disallow her to name other feelings that might seem out of character with her usual optimism. Give her permission to have all the feelings. Help her learn that it isn't wrong to be sad or mad sometimes.

- Avoid labeling her as the child who is always happy. While this may be true most of the time, it may not give her incentive to develop the other emotional-literacy skills she needs. She needs to learn to express all feelings so she can understand the feelings of others too.

- A child who has a very positive mood can be a catalyst to others for embracing and participating in changes at your program. For example, if she is excited to be moving to the four-year-old room, she will share that enthusiasm with peers who are also moving up but may be fearful of the change.

- Allow her to use her natural disposition where possible in the child care program. For example, let her use her eagerness to share something new with others, like doing a drama for parent night. Don't expect her to be cheerful all the time, but let her demonstrate her happiness when she is feeling it.

### Teach safety.

- A child high on positive mood may be more impulsive than a less optimistic child. He may not think that anything harmful or bad can happen to him.

He needs to have the same boundaries and limits that all children have so he learns self-regulation skills and impulse control.

- He is a child who is approachable and friendly. Help him learn to take a pause before going to new people. While you aren't squelching his natural tendency to be outgoing, you are giving him tools to make safe judgments about people he doesn't know yet.

### *Teach her the necessary skills to be more assertive.*

- Because she is happy-go-lucky, she may give in to a peer rather than taking a stand. While this can be a good trait at times, she could also be taken advantage of by others who know she will give in. For instance, it may not be worth it to her to fight over a favorite doll; however, if she has waited to use an activity center, it is appropriate that she gets her turn.

- It's important that adults do not send a message that the persona of sunniness is better or somehow more desirable than standing up for oneself. Help her to have the words to say what she needs. Dispel any stereotypes about what it means to be a "good girl" who doesn't make waves.

- Because this child tends not to complain, you may not know if she is being bullied or left out by others. As with all the children in your program, emotional literacy is critical to ongoing social-emotional development. If she needs to, help her practice phrases like "It's my turn now" or "I don't like it when you. . . ."

The natural disposition of a child to be happy and optimistic needs to be nurtured and valued like all temperament traits. You might think a child high on positive mood would not have struggles with friendship competencies, but being aware of each child's individual interactions with others, especially in play, will show you when he needs guidance from you.

## Story of Success

Raffi is a very cheerful nine-month-old. He has been in the infant room at Mt. Holyoke Child Care since birth. He is easy to care for because he usually only signals a need like eating or a diaper change with a fussy sound. His two teachers say that he always has a bright smile when they pick him up or call to him. Both teachers do a lot of "serve and return" with Raffi because of his pleasant mood, so there is a lot of cooing back and forth. He seems to give the whole infant room a positive feel.

# 12

## Guidance Strategies for Temperament Types— Putting the Pieces Together!

> Children come to us in all shapes and sizes, with personalities as diverse as they are. Our differences bring variety and excitement that teaches all of us adaptability and acceptance.

This book has explained the nine different temperament traits as well as behaviors that frequently accompany those traits. The strategies in each chapter are meant to provide you with tools to design a guidance plan for children who may be struggling to succeed in your setting. In this chapter, the view turns more globally at our approaches to challenging behaviors within the context of child differences.

## Guidance for Common Temperament Types

The three main temperament types of feisty, flexible, and fearful have combinations of traits that tend to represent some behaviors. As seen in chapter 1, these clusters of temperament traits are general classifications. One child may have more challenging behaviors than another because the environment he is in does not set him up for success as well as another child in a different setting.

### Strategy for Feisty

A child whose temperament traits cluster in the feisty temperament style has lots of energy and zest, which can sometimes translate into challenging behaviors. You will generally know when this child is happy or when this child is displeased with what is going on around him. He will tend to be low on adaptability, low on regularity, negative in mood, higher in sensitivity, and higher in intensity and activity level.

**Main strategy:** Anticipate reactions as much as possible to be proactive. Make plans for changes in schedules or staffing well ahead of time. Use fewer transitions during the day. Your flexibility will be your main tool in keeping challenging behaviors in check.

### Strategy for Flexible

Flexible means easy to get along with as a temperament cluster, so your guidance for this child is going to focus more on ensuring that she isn't too flexible in giving in to others and not expressing her own needs. A child in this temperament type is generally positive in mood, high in adaptability and approach, and low in intensity and sensitivity. She will typically be a joy to have around.

**Main strategy:** Be intentional in checking in with her to see how she is feeling about her relationships with others and her participation. She may hesitate to share a negative feeling, so help her understand that all feelings are welcome here and you are her ally.

### Strategy for Fearful

Children with the fearful temperament style tend to be slow to warm up. They need more time and more guidance from their caregiver to get used to a new situation or to new people, whether staff or peers. A child who is in the fearful style will be low on adaptability and will fall on the withdraw side of withdraw/approach. Because his nature is more hesitant, he will need to feel secure before he tries something new, so last-minute changes will likely invoke challenging behaviors.

**Main strategy:** Keep your routines and schedules as consistent as possible. Introduce changes slowly and let the child know you are there to support him if he needs it. Encourage independence by using a slow approach with him.

## Guidance for a Combination of Temperament Traits

Every child will come into your program with a combination of the nine temperament traits. He may be high, low, or in the middle on some or all of them. This will determine the clusters discussed in the section above. However, some combinations of traits more naturally go together. When these traits are combined, they can present challenges to you as the provider. Some combinations that you will likely see are described in the sections below.

## Strategy for Negative Mood and High Sensory Awareness

A child who tends toward a negative mood and also has high sensory awareness can show behaviors that center on his displeasure with the environment. He may be vocal when the room is too warm or too cold. He may refuse to eat something because he isn't familiar with it or he had it before and didn't like it. His sensory system will dictate his comfort according to his seven senses, and his tendency to see the negative side can overemphasize his sensory discomforts.

**Main strategy:** Try giving him more breaks throughout the day to keep his sensory system in better balance and prevent complaints. (See more strategies in chapters 10 and 11.)

## Strategy for High Activity Level and High Distractibility

When a child is very active, she will already have struggles staying on task or settling in one place for very long. If she also has difficulty staying focused, challenging behaviors can occur as she struggles to complete activities that you need for her to do in order to learn. She may also disrupt the play and concentration of others by joining and leaving games or activities quickly before finishing.

**Main strategy:** Blend a high interest area of hers (dolphins) into other areas of programming, like dramatic play (being a biologist), art (painting oceans and animals), and the reading nook (books on sea life). (See more strategies in chapters 3 and 4.)

## Strategy for High Intensity and High Activity Level

A child who reacts to the world around him with gusto and is very active at the same time could be frustrating to a provider who wants less energy given to every event and situation. The high intensity means the child will be louder and less tuned in to the moods and feelings of others, while with his high energy he may burst through and break up a group of children playing together. Other children might follow his lead in racing through the classroom, or they might get angry at him for disrupting an activity.

**Main strategy:** Find an outlet for the energy that uses the intensity as well. One idea might be to let this child conduct a marching band twice a day when he has the most unused energy. He can be the leader who marches loudly and even bangs something for a drum while everyone else gets to be in the parade too. (See more strategies in chapters 3 and 8.)

## Strategy for High Withdrawal and Low Adaptability

When a child is low on approachability and adaptability, she will have trouble with changes to staffing, new children, or any other differences in schedule or activities. Her behaviors will be displays of resistance and could include tantrums or other forms of refusals. Both withdrawal and low approachability make it harder for a child to build relationships with friends and adults.

**Main strategy:** Ease into changes slowly and give this child advance warning of major changes. (See more strategies in chapters 6 and 7.)

### Strategy for High Regularity and Low Adaptability

A child with high regularity and low adaptability can be rigid when it comes to the schedule, especially eating and napping. Low adaptability means he won't take to a change easily, and regularity means his body tells him, "It's noon, and I want to eat right now." This could result in meltdowns if the schedule is varied too much without warning.

**Main strategy:** Provide for a child's needs if you know the schedule is going to be off. Putting out a snack earlier, for example, can help prevent whining or crying when lunch is late. (See more strategies in chapters 7 and 9.)

### Low Persistence and High Distractibility

Low persistence means a child gives up easily when confronted with a challenge. Couple this with a lack of ability to stay tuned in or focused, and you will see behaviors ranging from frustration to acting out based on a lack of engagement. It is also frustrating for teachers to work with a child who won't complete a task or uses whining or complaining because she won't stay on task.

**Main strategy:** Offer fewer choices to a child. Build on the child's interests in the choices you do offer. (See more strategies in chapters 5 and 4.)

## Turning Negatives into Positives

Each of the temperament traits that has been examined in the previous chapters can present challenges to you as the early educator. Challenges happen when your schedule is disrupted, your activities are cut short, or children are at odds with one another. A lot of planning goes into a teacher's curriculum and programming each day. When the day does not go the way it was intended, goals are not met and sometimes learning is interrupted. Regardless of a child's dominant traits or temperament style, child care programs and classrooms will always have surprises and distractions from the daily routine because we are working with infants, toddlers, and preschoolers whose physical and emotional needs vary each day. Having a solid foundation in temperament gives the teacher a positive lens through which to see behavior, even challenging behavior, as part and parcel to the early childhood day! With strategies in place, we can diminish the impact of some of the behaviors as we continue to support children's social-emotional development.

## Reframing Dispositions

Rather than seeing what is negative about a child's natural disposition, trying to reframe dispositions to see the positive will help both the child and the adults reach more successful outcomes.

**Activity Level:** Look at the energy the child brings to your program. Think about how she boosts other children's enthusiasm. High activity level can be seen as enthusiasm and dynamo. Low activity level can be a calming influence to others.

**Distractibility:** This can mean creativity and a different way of looking at the world. Embrace the new ways this child sees life. Try looking at your program through his eyes and see what he is seeing when he isn't focused on your story or your directions. Maybe everyone will want to see the red bird outside the window.

**Persistence:** On the high end, persistence means a child sticks with it, follows through, and finishes. This is a help to other children who need to finish tasks too. On the low end, a child can be creative and want to do things differently, moving back and forth easily in new activities.

**Adaptability:** On one end is a child who is highly flexible and who goes with the flow, making change and transitions easy. On the other end, you have a child who likes to think things through and decide on his own time about new things, which gives you the opportunity to see your changes through a child's eyes.

**Approach/Withdrawal:** A flexible and friendly child is a wonderful addition to child care. He helps other children with social skills. A child who is less outgoing teaches us to observe each child according to his mood and not use a cookie-cutter approach.

**Intensity:** Having a child who brings gusto in all he does is energizing! This is a fun child who will brings lots of energy to the whole program. If he has less intensity, learn to appreciate the way he sits back and watches with less emotion. Some days that will be just what everyone needs.

**Regularity:** A child who is on a regular schedule is rarely out of sorts. She transitions well and doesn't fuss much. A child who is less regular takes to changes easily and reminds us to keep our schedules and routines consistent.

**Sensory Threshold:** Whether a child is high or low on sensory awareness, we get a picture from him of how our environment is working for the children. This is an important awareness for teachers because it is easy to get used to what we see every day. A child can help us hear or touch or smell what we may be missing!

**Mood:** Whether pessimistic or optimistic, a child's viewpoint helps us see things from a different angle. We are learning, too, and we want to model to children a willingness to adapt when our environment isn't as friendly or open as it should be to everyone.

## Considering the Unique Child

When you begin to see a personality trait in a positive light, you can begin to cherish the child for the diversity that she brings to your program. For instance, a child who has high intensity may sometimes be loud at the wrong times, but she also brings great energy and gusto to your group activities! How boring it would be if all children responded in the same way all the time. Teachers might joke how the one child they could really use a break from is never absent, but in reality, that child is often the one they have the most favorite stories about when they go home at night.

Each temperament trait will manifest uniquely in every child. While we know that each disposition has general behaviors associated with it, we also know that a temperament trait is not the picture of the whole child. Each child comes to you with a family of origin, a culture, a language, perhaps trauma, and most certainly unique experiences. How the temperament trait influences behavior also has much to do with the goodness of fit in the environment and in the child's relationships with caring providers.

Children come to us wired a particular way due to genetics. The early educator can guide a child according to his dominant temperament traits with strategies that give him tools for making friends and developing to his fullest potential. We want to honor all children as unique individuals and promote their particular strengths and personalities.

## Putting Strategies to Use

The strategies in this book are laid out for the reader by temperament trait, temperament style, and finally by combinations of dominant temperament traits. Considering each child's unique temperament needs, you can stop a challenging behavior from escalating or becoming a pattern of behavior for a child as the proactive strategies in this book can help you guide her into more positive behaviors. The strategies can also help you to keep a challenge from escalating or becoming a pattern of behavior. You have successfully prevented challenging behaviors when the child has learned and practiced new and different behaviors guided by you.

Throughout this book, we have explored the high and low end of each temperament trait. For any child care teacher, depending on her own dominant temperament traits, each disposition can present challenges if you don't have the tools at hand to be successful. And what can seem difficult for one provider might be a preference for another, again depending on her own temperament and the mix of children she has in her program. As you work with young children, the better you will get to know each child individually and the more you will be able to understand his unique temperament and what he needs from your setting to be most successful.

The nine temperament traits and three temperament types bring a mix of personalities into your programs. You will naturally be drawn to children who are easier for you to interact with based on your own temperament type. There is no good trait or bad trait. All traits are natural and wonderful, particularly when you have tools to provide goodness of fit. Enjoy the journey!

# References

Allen, K. Eileen, and Glynnis E. Cowdery. 2012. *The Exceptional Child: Inclusion in Early Childhood Education*. 7th ed. Belmont, CA: Wadsworth/Cengage Learning.

Berk, Laura E. 2013. *Child Development*. Boston: Pearson.

Croft, Cindy. 2007. *The Six Keys: Strategies for Promoting Children's Mental Health in Early Childhood Programs*. Farmington, MN: Sparrow Media Group.

Gartrell, Dan. 2012. *Education for a Civil Society: How Guidance Teaches Young Children Democratic Life Skills*. Washington, DC: National Association for the Education of Young Children.

Gilliam, Walter S., Angela N. Maupin, Chin R. Reyes, Maria Accavitti, and Frederick Shic. 2016. *Do Early Educators' Implicit Biases Regarding Sex and Race Relate to Behavior Expectations and Recommendations of Preschool Expulsions and Suspensions?* New Haven, CT: Yale University Child Study Center. https://medicine.yale.edu/childstudy/zigler/publications/Preschool%20 Implicit%20Bias%20Policy%20Brief_final_9_26_276766_5379_v1.pdf.

Greenspan, Stanley I., and Ira Glovinsky. 2007. *Children and Babies with Mood Swings: New Insights for Parents and Professionals*. Bethesda, MD: ICDL.

HHS, and ED (US Departments of Health and Human Services and Education). 2014. *Policy Statement on Expulsion and Suspension Policies in Early Childhood Settings*. https://www2.ed.gov/policy/gen/guid/school-discipline /policy-statement-ece-expulsions-suspensions.pdf.

NAEYC (National Association for the Education of Young Children). 2020. "Three Core Considerations of DAP." NAEYC. www.naeyc.org/resources /topics/dap/3-core-considerations. Accessed July 17.

Technical Assistance Center on Social Emotional Intervention for Young Children. www.challengingbehavior.org.

# Resources

*Caring for Young Children with Special Needs* by Cindy Croft

Center for Inclusive Child Care. www.inclusivechildcare.org

Center on the Social and Emotional Foundations for Early Learning. http://csefel.vanderbilt.edu

Infant Toddler Temperament Tool (IT³) by the Center for Early Childhood Mental Health Consultation, an Innovation and Improvement Project funded by the Office of Head Start. https://www.ecmhc.org/temperament

National Association for the Education of Young Children (NAEYC). www.naeyc.org

Zero to Three. www.zerotothree.org

# Index

less preferred activities and, 55
as part of feisty temperament type, 69
play skills of, 66
relationships with, 64, 65–66
teaching strategies for, 66–68
decreasing sensory stimulation in classroom
and, 16
described, 3, 55
disposition reframing, 183
environment and, 55–56, 61
feisty temperament type and, 8
group times and, 33–34, 63
guidance strategies for children with high
activity level and high, 181
guidance strategies for children with low persistence and high, 182
distress tantrums, 150
dramatic play, 44, 66, 122, 128, 160–161

E
early childhood educators
child development lens to understand temperament, 25
curriculum as guide for, 58
extent of teacher-directed activities, 58
importance of seeing each temperament trait
in positive light, 184
intentionality in giving directions or instructions, 62
knowing each child as individual, 21
persistence of child's temperament traits and,
14
responsiveness to child's needs, 16
setting stage for positive behaviors with body
language and words, 27
temperament of
behaviors of children and, 13
goodness of fit and, 35–36
perception of others and, 25
understanding own, 9–12
early childhood educators' relationships with
children
with high activity level, 42–43
with high adaptability, 86–87
with high approach, 100–101
with high distractibility, 59–60
with high intensity, 116, 118–119, 124–125
with high persistence, 73
with high regularity, 136–137
with high sensory awareness, 151
with low activity level, 50
with low adaptability, 91
with low distractibility, 65–66
with low intensity, 127
with low persistence, 78

with low regularity, 142
with low sensory awareness, 158
with negative mood, 168–169, 171
with positive mood, 174–175
with withdrawal (low approach), 107–108
easy/easygoing temperament type. *See* flexible
temperament type
emotional literacy
children with high intensity, 121
children with high persistence, 75
children with high sensory awareness, 153–154
children with low intensity, 126, 129, 130–131
children with low regularity, 145–146
children with low sensory awareness and, 162
children with negative mood, 170, 171
children with positive mood, 176, 177
children with withdrawal (low approach), 111
language skills to support, 75, 94
emotional regularity, 134
emotional sensitivity
children with high, 150, 152
described, 148–149
encouragement, 47, 53
energy. *See* activity level
environment
adaptability and changes in, 84
control over, by children with high sensory
awareness, 154
emotional, 34, 56
physical
adaptability and changes in environment,
32–33
assessing, 33
boundaries, 32, 47
calming, 2, 155
children with low persistence and, 80
clutter in, 61, 79
distractibility and, 55–56, 61
fidget boxes, 161
goodness of fit and, 35, 36–37
grouping like centers together, 61
importance of, 32
influence on temperament of, 2, 15
large, open spaces, 35
lighting in, 155, 156
as preventative tool, 32
quiet areas, 32, 34, 46, 121, 155
sensory and sand tables, 160
sensory boxes, 161
sensory input in, 58
take-a-break spaces, 16, 32, 62, 122
tools for children with high activity level,
34
sensory
area with few distractions, 155

routines to build biological regulation, 47
waiting before acting to support self-regulation, 88, 103
impulsiveness, children with high
feisty temperament type and, 41
learning to regulate, 23
infants
activity level, 39, 41
adaptability, 4, 86
intensity, 4, 116
mood, 165
regularity, 133, 134, 135, 140
sensory awareness, 152
withdrawal (low approach), 98
instructions, giving, 62
intensity
children with high
behaviors of, 116–119
changes in schedules/routines and, 24
described, 115, 116
feisty temperament type and, 41
inside and outside voices and, 37
play skills of, 119–121
relationships with others, 116, 118–119, 120, 124–125
teaching strategies for, 121–125
children with low
behaviors of, 125–127
described, 115–116, 125
play skills of, 128–129
relationships with others, 127–128
teaching strategies for, 129–131
described, 4, 115
disposition reframing, 183
feisty temperament type and, 8, 83, 125
flexible temperament and, 125, 126
guidance strategies for children with high
activity level and high, 181

## L

labeling
children with high distractibility, 56
children with high persistence, 69–70, 76
children with high sensory awareness, 155
children with negative mood, 167–168, 172
children with positive mood, 167, 176
children with withdrawal (low approach), 113
inappropriately, 22
pitfalls of, 19–20, 21, 23
respecting children and, 34
language, ix, 27
language skills
children with high persistence, 74
children with high sensory awareness, 156
children with low distractibility, 66

children with low intensity, 126, 128, 130–131
children with withdrawal (low approach), 108
friendships and, 65–66
play and, 44, 51, 66, 92, 101
to support emotional literacy, 75, 94

## M

mastery play, 92–93
mood
children with negative
behaviors of, 167–168
described, 165, 166–167
play skills of, 169
relationships with others, 168–169, 171
teaching strategies for, 170–172
children with positive
behaviors, 173–174, 176–177
described, 165–166, 173
play skills of, 175
relationships with others, 174–175
teaching strategies for, 175–177
described, 4, 165
disposition reframing, 183–184
guidance strategies for children with high
sensory awareness and negative, 181
motor coordination, 51
motor planning, 51

## N

National Association for the Education of Young
Children (NANCE), 31
noise
children with high distractibility and, 57, 61, 62
children with high sensory awareness and, 156
children with low persistence and, 80
quiet space/time, children with low sensory
threshold for sound, 34
structuring environment to modulate, 16

## O

observation
assessment of physical environment and, 33
using, to track behaviors and *see* development
of pattern, 29
obtain function of behaviors, 26
olfactory sense, 149, 154

## P

parents. *See* primary caregivers
persistence
children with high
behaviors, 71–72
described, 69–70